THE MESSAGE OF
ABRAHAM
His Life, Virtues, and Mission

THE MESSAGE OF
ABRAHAM

HIS LIFE, VIRTUES, AND MISSION

İbrahim Canan

Translated by Jessica Özalp

Light

New Jersey

Published by The Light, Inc.
26 Worlds Fair Dr. Unit C
Somerset, New Jersey, 08873, USA

www.thelightpublishing.com

Library of Congress Cataloging-in-Publication Data

Canan, Ibrahim.
  [Hz. Ibrahim'den mesajlar. English]
  The message of Abraham : his life, virtues, and mission / Ibrahim Canan ;
  translated by Jessica Ozalp. -- 1st ed.
      p. cm.
  Includes bibliographical references and index.
  ISBN-13: 978-1-59784-075-0
  1. Abraham (Biblical patriarch) in the Koran. 2. Prophets, Pre-Islamic. I. Title.
  BP133.7.A27C3613 2007
  297.2'463--dc22

                                        2007001097

Printed by
Çağlayan A.Ş., Izmir - Turkey
May 2007

TABLE OF CONTENTS

PREFACE

Praise to God Almighty for making the edition of this book a reality. I would like to briefly explain how this book came to be as a result of the hope-inspiring growth of dialogue and tolerance initiatives among members of the Abrahamic faiths. It originated as a paper titled "Messages of Prophet Abraham in the Qur'an," presented in Urfa in 1997 at the First Abrahamic Symposium organized by Harran University and SURKAV. The paper was later expanded and published by Şule Publications in 1998 in Istanbul as "The Messages of Prophet Abraham." Soon after this, in 2000, a second interfaith dialogue symposium was organized in Şanlıurfa by the Istanbul-based Journalists and Writers Foundation, this time on an international scale. I participated in this symposium with another paper called "Family Ethics of Prophet Abraham," which included some material from the book regarding ethics, reorganized and with new sections (these changes are also reflected in the second edition of the book.) My interpretation of some Qur'anic verses related to Abraham, approached from an ethical perspective and my concordant proposition of a framework for an educational system drew attention.

The concept of dialogue, not only between different religions but also different cultures and civilizations, has taken on many new aspects since 1997. At that time some groups viewed this with suspicion, but although they were quick to criticize and accuse, today the concept and its importance has been accepted and recognized by several well-represented segments of society. It has even entered Turkish governmental policy. While emphasizing my belief that the results expected from these dialogue initiatives will be achieved, I would like to point out that the peace and well-being of the whole of humanity, not just one group, depends on there being understanding and peace among the followers of Abrahamic traditions.

I have no doubt that this and similar works will help strengthen the foundation for the dialogue and tolerance that is needed for world peace to be established.

I hope to see new works in a similar vein, and I wish to thank The Light Publishing for their careful attention to detail in producing this book.

İbrahim Canan

THE IMPORTANCE OF THE
PROPHET ABRAHAM

Prophet Abraham's name appears 69 times in the Qur'an. This makes it the second most-often repeated after that of Prophet Moses, which is found 136 times. This frequent occurrence of his name, and the fact that a chapter (*sura*) is named after him, is Qur'anic proof of the importance of Abraham in both the history of humankind and the religion of Islam.[1] This being the case, we should analyze the origin of the importance placed on this figure.

When we examine in detail the verses of the Qur'an regarding Abraham we come face to face with the exemplary and outstanding characteristics which compose his personality, and some of the very important services that he performed.

One of the most unique attributes of this elevated character that is relevant to our day is his being a unifying figure among all the revealed religions. Fakhreddin Razi said of Prophet Abraham, "All traditions and faiths agree in his virtue. Even in pre-Islamic Arabia the polytheist Arabs also recognized his virtue, and felt honored to be his descendants."[2]

He is at the crossroads of the three monotheistic religions. The Jews, Christians, and Muslims are united in proclaiming his high station, and in order to get a share of his wisdom and to take part in his honor, they associate themselves with him. For example, in the Torah it is said of Abraham,

> The Lord said unto Abraham, "I will make of you a great nation, and I will bless you and make your name great; and you shall be a blessing; and I will bless them that bless you, and curse

him that curses you, and in you shall all families of the Earth be blessed." (Genesis 12, 1-3)

In a different verse, the Torah says: "As for me, this is my covenant with you: You will be the father of many nations" (Genesis 17, 4). According to a common understanding among Jewish rabbis, Prophet Abraham is "the father of all people who receive guidance." It is for this reason that if someone accepted their faith and received a Hebrew name, it was "son of Abraham."[3]

Abraham is given no less importance among Christians. In a verse from St. Paul's letter to the Romans, it is written, "Abraham is father of all of us" (Romans 4, 17) and another verse explains: "It was not through law that Abraham and his offspring received the promise that he would be heir of the world, but through the righteousness that comes by faith" (Romans 4,13). In short, both Christians and Jews recognize Prophet Abraham as a great symbol of faith.[4]

In the Qur'an, as a response to the claim by some Jews and Christians over this important model of faith, both of which say "Abraham is one of us," it is stated that he was neither a Jew nor a Christian, but rather Muslim (one who submits to the one God):

> O People of the Book! Why do you dispute concerning Abraham (whether he was a Jew or a Christian), when both the Torah and the Gospel were not sent down save after him? Will you not ever use your reason? Indeed, you are such people that you (do not use your reason but) you dispute concerning a matter about which you have knowledge (in order not to admit the truth); why, then, should you dispute on a matter about which you have no knowledge. God knows, but you know not. Abraham was not a Jew, nor a Christian; but he was a Muslim, one pure of faith and submitted to God with a sound heart. He was never of the idolaters. (Al Imran 3:65-67)

> Or do you claim that Abraham, Ishmael, Isaac, Jacob and the Prophets among Jacob's descendants were "Jews" or "Christians"? (O Messenger,) say (to them): Do you know better, or does God? (Baqara 2:140)

In the Qur'an Abraham represents such a unique wisdom that the greatness of the honor of being related to him makes it worth debating to whom he belongs. This is not denied in the Qur'an. The claim of Jews and of Christians to carry on the Abrahamic tradition is not accepted, as they haven't been able to keep their original religion:

> Or do you claim that Abraham, Ishmael, Isaac, Jacob and the Prophets who were raised in the tribes were "Jews" or "Christians?" Say (to them): "Do you know better, or does God?" (They know well that any of the Prophets were neither "Jews" nor "Christians," but they conceal the truth.) Who is greater in wrongdoing than he who conceals the testimony he has from God? God is never unaware and unmindful of what you do. (Al Imran 3:68)

As we have seen, the Qur'an states both Abraham was Muslim (one who submits to the will of the One God) and that Prophet Muhammad and those who accept his prophethood were following the religion of Abraham. Furthermore, in one verse it is mentioned that the word "Muslim" was used to describe the true believers by Abraham long ago.[5]

Indeed, Abraham's was quite a multifaceted personality. He was the builder of the Ka'ba, the one who instituted the Hajj (Pilgrimage); the one declared monotheism,[6] who started the systematic struggle against polytheism and originated its methodology and logic; he was the founder of many initiatives designed to protect the health of society and much more. After building the Ka'ba he declared Mecca a sacred city and within its borders prohibited the spilling of blood, as well as hunting, cutting down trees, destroying foliage, and uprooting vegetation. In so doing, he was making the first of humankind's serious decisions about environmental issues and became an expert in this area which is first among humanity's modern-day concerns.

In our world, which is quickly becoming a global village, Prophet Abraham, beloved first of all by monotheists but also by all the religions, is a personality that can make important contributions toward forming a world community.

His personality, historical mission, service, and messages must certainly be revived and updated, so that Prophet Abraham may once again be familiar to us in all aspects.

THE NECESSITY OF EMULATING THE PROPHET ABRAHAM: HIS EXCELLENT EXAMPLE

In the Qur'an it is stated that he is a good example for all people:

> Indeed you have an excellent example to follow in Abraham and those in his company . . . (Mumtahina 60:4)

In addition, in the Qur'an Prophet Muhammad is commanded to follow Prophet Abraham:

> And lastly, We have revealed to you, (O Messenger,) to follow the way of Abraham as one of pure faith (free from unbelief, associating partners with God and hypocrisy.) He was never of the idolaters . . . (Nahl 16:123)

The following verse declares that this command was fulfilled:

> (O Messenger) declare: "Assuredly, my Lord has guided me to a straight highway, that is a right religion with no crookedness at all, the way of Abraham based on pure faith (free from unbelief, associating partners with God and hypocrisy.) He was never of those who associated partners with God."(An'am 6:161)

In fact, a commandment that may seem to be specific to the Prophet is actually binding on all Muslims. These two verses suffice to make it known that the whole of the Prophet's community is subject to follow Abraham's religion of strict monotheism until the Day of Judgment. But in another verse, the Qur'an addresses to further draw the attention of the community to this and to make clear that it is imperative that they follow the nation of Abraham:

> (O Messenger) say you: "God speaks the truth." Therefore fol-
> low the way of Abraham as people of pure faith (free from unbe-
> lief, associating partners with God and hypocrisy.) He was never
> of the idolaters. (Al Imran 3:95)

Prophet Muhammad, the Messenger of God, also says, "I was sent with the religion of absolute monotheism, which is easy and tolerant."[7]

Yet another verse encourages us toward the Abrahamic religion by praising those who follow him:

> Who is better in religion than he who has submitted his whole
> being to God, purely seeking His good pleasure as one devot-
> ed to doing good, fully aware that God always sees him, and he
> who follows the way of Abraham as one of pure faith (free
> from unbelief, associating partners with God and hypocrisy).
> God took Abraham for a close, trusted friend. (Nisa 4:125)

Also, this verse admonishes those who do not follow Prophet Abraham's faith:

> Who (therefore) shrinks from the Way of Abraham, save him
> who makes himself a fool? (Baqara 2:130)

What is this Abrahamic religion which the Blessed Prophet Muhammad and all Muslims, until the Last Day, are called to follow? What are its characteristics and basic principles?

In this work I will try to answer these questions, taking as a reference the explanations found in the Qur'anic verses related to Prophet Abraham.

I look to God for assistance.

PART ONE

The Life of the Prophet Abraham

There is no information in the Qur'an about Prophet Abraham's place of birth. Neither do history books give us satisfactory answers about this. Some of the details of his life are given in the Torah and the Bible. At any rate, there are many conflicting views today about the birthplace of Prophet Abraham. According to some of these, he was born in the vicinity of modern day Iraq.[1]

According to some traditions his birthplace is Harran.[2] Harran is an old residential area and was a major center of civilization, located about 25 miles from Urfa, Turkey. It is claimed that Prophet Abraham's father was from Harran, and after the birth he brought his son to Babylon.[3]

There is a common belief in Urfa since ancient times that Prophet Abraham was born there; indeed there exists a cave they call "the birth cave of Abraham," which is visited as a blessed place.

From a Qur'anic perspective the place where Abraham was born carries no importance; thus the birthplace is not made clear. In the holy book, importance is given to the messages Abraham brought.

As for the time when Prophet Abraham lived, this is much less clear. According to the tradition cited in the Encyclopedia of Islam, he was born 1,263 years after the Flood, or 3,337 years after the world was created.[4] Surely these are not exact dates. With the same qualification,[5] I would like to relate another tradition from Ibn Sa'd: "Between Prophet Adam and Prophet Abraham 2,000 years had passed, and between Prophet Abraham and Prophet Muhammad 2,469 years."[6]

In the Qur'an the close connection between Prophet Abraham and Prophet Lot is mentioned, showing that they were contemporaries. Yet it gives no information about exactly how many years separated them from Prophet Adam or Prophet Noah before them, or Prophet Jesus or Prophet Muhammad after them. Instead, the Qur'an gives importance to the role they played in human history, meaning the messages they brought, the way they taught the faith, the crookedness and hedonism their peoples had fallen into, the struggles they went through to correct them, the resistance the people showed against them, the accusations and evil leveled against these prophets, the patience and submission to God, the persistence shown by the prophets, the miracles they performed, and at the end of all their efforts, the people's acceptance of the straight path or the way of destruction. Instead of details regarding time and place, greater insight of the above-mentioned issues is given in the Qur'an. In fact, the guidelines that will bring people happiness in this world and the Hereafter lie in these lessons. This is the case, not only for Prophet Abraham, but for all the prophets.

The lack of specific information explained above also applies to the personal lives of the prophets. That is, in the Qur'an the events in their lives, without clarifying what came first or what came later, are described. For instance, although there are very many stories about Prophet Abraham, no clear chronological order is given for them.

Because the need has arisen, I will try to put in order the events of Abraham's life which are mentioned in the Qur'an, referring to historical narrations, traditions, and interpretations. As I know these may not always be totally accurate, I will begin by saying, "God knows best."

His Struggles

Prophet Abraham's father was an idol maker. He gave the idols he had made to his sons to sell in the marketplace. Prophet Abraham, sitting beside his wares, shouted,

"Doesn't anyone want to buy these idols which have no power to help or harm?" His brothers came home having sold their idols, but Abraham returned with the idols, as he had been unable to sell them.[7] Then he invited his father to the right way:

> "O my father! Why do you worship that which neither hears nor sees, nor can in anything avail you?" (Maryam 19:42)

Later Abraham went to the building where the idols were kept. This was a large hall, and all the idols were facing the direction of the door. In the center was a large idol, flanked by smaller idols, lined up according to size. This line of idols reached to the door. Gifts of food had been placed in front of the idols. The idol worshippers had put them there saying, "these offerings we place before our gods will win us blessings, and when we return we will eat it." Abraham, seeing the idols and the food in front of them, said,

> "Will you not eat?"
> "What is the matter with you that you do not speak?" (Saffat 37:91-92)

Then Abraham fell upon them, striking them with all his strength. After this exhorted his people and warned them. He said, "Do you worship things that you yourselves have carved, while it is God Who has created you and all that you do?" (Saffat 37:93-96) The people seized him, imprisoned him in a house and began to collect firewood. They approached this task with such zeal that a woman who became ill prayed for health, promising to collect wood for Abraham if she got well. When a huge amount of wood had been collected they built a fire with it. The fire began burning fearfully. It was so great that birds could not fly overhead without being burned by the intense heat and flames. They came to the building where Prophet Abraham was and took him up to the roof. He raised his face to Heaven. The sky, mountains and angels begged, "Oh Lord! Abraham will be burned in following Your way (help him!)" God answered, "I know him; if he asks your help, assist him." Abraham, lifting his head, said,

"Oh my Lord! You are alone in the Heavens, as I am alone on
the Earth. There is none besides me who serves You faithfully.
God is enough for me, and He is the best Protector."

They threw him into the fire. Gabriel commanded the fire, "O
fire, be cool and peaceful for Abraham!" Ibn Abbas explains that if
the command "Be cool!" had not been followed by "Be peaceful!"
Abraham would have been frozen inside the fire. On that day all
fires on the face of the Earth were extinguished.

When the fire had died, they came to see Abraham. They found
him with a man, his head on the man's lap, as the man wiped the sweat
from his face. It was said that the stranger was the angel of shade.
God had blessed the fire, and all the children of Adam benefited from
it. They took Abraham from the fire and brought him to the king's
court. He had never been before the king and he spoke with him.

This story is narrated from Suddi by Ibn Abi Hatim. In the
classic books there is no sign of a desire to put into a chronological order the events of Prophet Abraham's life, which are told piece
by piece in the Qur'an. The tradition related above is a portion from
the longest and most detailed of those in *Al-Durr al-Mansur*.

According to the story favored by Ibn al-Athir, around the
time of Abraham's birth the soothsayers came to Nimrod, telling
him that from his town would come one named Abraham who would
defy his religion, break the idols, and end the king's reign; they told
him the month and year when this would occur, and based on this
news Nimrod took some precautions.[8]

Hamdi Yazir of Elmali leaves aside the details of Prophet
Abraham's birth and childhood, instead focusing on the life of Prophet
Abraham from the beginning of his mission, describing these stages.
He invited people to the religion; first his father, then his people, and
the ruler of the time (Nimrod). After that, he struggled against idolatry, and destroyed the idols. In return, his people attempted to execute him by fire. In a later stage of his life, he had to sacrifice his son.

Hamdi Yazir explains that by his success in these tests, Abraham
won God's pleasure; God had accepted his prayer for himself and

his generation, ". . . Grant me a most true and virtuous renown among posterity" (Shu'ara 26:84) and that for this reason, he was loved by the idol worshippers of Arabia as well as by Jews and Christians.[9]

Being a crucial period of Prophet Abraham's life, we may ask whether his struggle with Nimrod came before or after his attempted execution by fire. This is rather unclear. But according to one tradition by Ibn Sa'd, it was before, and further, he spent 7 years imprisoned by the king. The same passage adds the following information: "Prophet Abraham's mother tongue was Aramaic. He emigrated from Babylon to Damascus (in Syria). When he got to the Euphrates River, God changed his language to Hebrew. Nimrod, to prevent his escape, sent men in pursuit of him, telling them not to allow any Aramaic speakers past the borders. Since Prophet Abraham spoke Hebrew, they were not able to recognize and capture him. At the time of this emigration he was 37 years of age."

Prophet Abraham undertook this migration together with his wife Sarah. They came to Harran and stayed there for some time. They moved from there to Egypt and later back to Damascus, and entering Sab[10] near the Bayt al-Maqdis area; he dug a well and constructed there a small house of prayer. In time he again suffered great difficulties at the hands of the people. Abandoning that place, he went down to a place called Katt or Kitt.[11] Making a well, he settled there. The well of Sab dried up when Abraham left, and repenting of their terrible behavior, the people called him to return; but he did not. A hero of mercy, Prophet Abraham did not act according to the wrongs they had done, but told them what they needed to do to have the water flow again. When they followed these instructions they again benefited from the well's water; when they ignored them it dried up again.[12]

In his new location he gained much wealth and many servants. By the time he received his prophetic mission and the title *Halilullah*, "Friend of God," he had 300 slaves. To show his gratitude to God he freed them all. These newly freed people submitted themselves to the will of God and Abraham's message, and stayed by his side.

Again according to Ibn Sa'd, Prophet Abraham traveled to Mecca three times. The first visit was commanded by God; he went on the divine steed Buraq. Gabriel himself showed the way. On this journey his two year old son Ishmael rode in front of him in the saddle, and his wife Hagar behind him. When he arrived in Mecca he left his family near where the Ka'ba stands today, and returned to Damascus.[13]

The second time, the purpose of his journey was to visit his family. When he arrived he learned that his wife had died. He returned without being able to see his son Ishmael. This was because Ishmael was not in Mecca, and Abraham had only received permission for the journey from his other wife, Sarah, on condition that he would not linger there, but return immediately.

The third time Abraham came to Mecca he performed the first Hajj (pilgrimage) and called all people to pilgrimage; all those who heard accepted the call and joined him. The first pilgrims were the tribe of Jurhum, who all accepted Islam. They were followed by the Amalica.[14]

The firstborn of Prophet Abraham was Ishmael, the son of Hagar. When Ishmael was born Prophet Abraham was 90 years old. According to one tradition, 30 years later Isaac was born. When Sarah died, he married a woman named Kantura from the tribe of Canaan. He had 4 children with her. His fourth marriage produced seven more children. Thus, Prophet Abraham fathered 13 children. This tradition even mentions the names of all the children.[15] In Tabari's narration, Kantura had 6 children by Abraham, and the fourth wife Hajur had 5 sons.[16] According to this tradition all 13 children were sons.

At this point it would be helpful to explain when Prophet Abraham given his wealth. Based on some Qur'anic verses, Islamic scholars agree that his wealth and property were awarded after Prophet Abraham had passed many difficult tests and trials, such as breaking the idols and being asked to sacrifice his son. Likewise, some scholars approach this verse with a similar interpretation:

> Do you not consider he who remonstrated with Abraham about
> his Lord (in defiance of Him) because of the kingdom God has
> granted him? (Baqara 2:258)

They take the pronoun "him" in this verse to refer to Abraham, meaning, "Are you not aware of that king who argued with Abraham about his Sustainer (out of jealousy), simply because God has granted (Abraham) wealth (or power)?" From this interpretation it is understood that Abraham became the owner of wealth and property after the incident of the fire and his emigration. The fact that when he invited people to the hajj, it was so easily accepted by the Jurhums first, then the Amalicas, and then all the people who had heard might serve as a proof that he became wealthy and powerful later on. In addition, his having enough wealth to free 300 slaves at once when prophethood was given to him, and in particular his cooperation in the struggle against polytheism with those freedmen who had surrendered themselves to God and accepted his mission all strengthen the likelihood that he received the prophethood after his emigration and struggles with Nimrod mentioned in the verse. God knows best.

As there was no one to be found who believed in Prophet Abraham at the time of the fire incident, it is highly unlikely that he commanded any wealth at that time. It seems more likely that Abraham, who was 37 at the time of emigration and who died at age 200, led the campaign to weaken and remove Nimrod in his later years. But this does not mean this struggle had not existed from the beginning. Also, by "struggle against Nimrod" I do not intend to refer only to that meeting mentioned in the Qur'an, which seems likely to have happened before the emigration.

THE STAGES OF HIS LIFE

I will give some figures and information regarding the stages of Prophet Abraham's life according to various traditions; however, I should remind readers that there is no reliable evidence for the accuracy of this information.

- Prophet Abraham was the son of Tarah, and was the fore-father of Prophet Noah, who sprang from his line 10 generations later.[17]
- When he was contemplating the stars, Abraham was 15 months of age.[18]
- His disagreement with his tribe and his inviting them to the right path probably happened after he reached puberty. When news of this came to Nimrod he threw Abraham in jail for 7 years.[19]
- When he was thrown into the fire he was 16 years old.[20]
- He was 37 when he made his emigration.[21]
- When Sarah conceived Isaac she was 90, and Prophet Abraham was 120.[22]
- According to those who claim that the son who was to be sacrificed was Isaac, the order to sacrifice him came in Damascus, 2 miles from Kudus. According to those who say it was Ishmael, the order came in Mecca.[23]
- According to Tabari's narrations, which contain conflicting information, the son who was to be sacrificed was Isaac, not Ishmael, and he was 16 at the time. His mother, on hearing the news, spent 2 days sick in bed, and died of grief on the third. The same source says Sarah was 127 years old at the time of her death.[24]
- After spreading his religion in the areas of Palestine and the Hijaz, Prophet Abraham returned to Damascus, and died there at 200 years of age.[25]

An Uncertainty and an Approximation

In telling the story of Prophet Abraham's life, there are some points which have remained unknown to date. One of these is when Prophet Abraham had his argument with Nimrod.

First I should say that Nimrod's name does not appear in the Qur'an. However, scholars and historians agree that the king with whom Prophet Abraham argued about God was Nimrod. Although there is no disagreement about this, the question remains whether the incident occurred before or after the fire incident.[26]

The verse which refers to the breaking of the idols shows that Abraham was not well known until he was about to break the idols: *Some said: "We heard a young man speak against them, who is called Abraham"* (Anbiya 21:60). Therefore it is less likely that his argument with Nimrod was before this. Even the fact that due to his father Azar's closeness to Nimrod no one was able to harass Abraham until that time makes it seem that he had a life of comfort and freedom until this incident. But it could be that Nimrod took interest in Abraham after hearing complaints about the breaking of the idols, and then after losing the argument threw him into jail, and seeing finally that jail did not change Abraham's mind, ordered the execution by fire.

There is another interpretation—put forward by a minority of scholars—which supports the theory that the argument came before the fire incident. According to this view, the following verse refers to Abraham with the word "kingdom":

> Do you not consider he who remonstrated with Abraham about his Lord (in defiance of Him) because of the kingdom God has granted him? (Baqara 2:258)

In this version, then, Nimrod suggested the debate out of self-confidence, wanting to save his authority by defeating Abraham in public, thereby diminishing Abraham's growing influence. But besides the fact that the majority reject this, another detail about the fire incident weakens this theory. That detail is that when he was thrown into the fire he was the only one with faith, and as of yet had no following.[27]

Thus, since no believers in Prophet Abraham could be found, there must have been no "kingdom" that would threaten Nimrod's throne. Therefore the authority/kingdom mentioned in the verse must be Nimrod's. If we keep in mind that according to what is said by Almighty God in the Qur'an, all things, all blessings and difficulties—whether given to good people or evil, to Nimrod or to

Abraham—come with the permission and knowledge of the Creator of all, then it is reasonable that to think that Nimrod's kingship could be referred to as "God-given."

In this case, according to some scholars, "Nimrod had become arrogant with the power that was given him by God, and had gone beyond his limits. He called Abraham in order to question and defeat him, and had the dispute which is summarized in the Qur'an; but when he could not silence Abraham he followed in the footsteps of all those throughout history who have been exposed by the light of the truth; he used force, throwing him into prison."

If this incarceration really happened (it is not mentioned in the Qur'an), it seems more likely that it happened before the incident of the fire. Nevertheless, the "death by fire" was a punishment related to the breaking of the idols. In this case, since the prison episode is not mentioned in the Qur'an, it is possible to say that after the breaking of the idols the decision for execution by fire was made, yet in order to make this a glorious celebration, a period of time was set for the preparations, and meanwhile Prophet Abraham was kept in jail. Moreover, since many small incidents from Prophet Abraham's life are not mentioned in the Qur'an, it is reasonable that this incarceration could have been left out because of its relative unimportance in comparison to the attempted execution and resulting emigration. The dispute between Abraham and Nimrod is given as follows:

> Do you not consider he who remonstrated with Abraham about his Lord (in defiance of Him) because of the kingdom God has granted him? When Abraham declared, "My Lord is He Who gives life and He who causes death," he retorted: "I also give life and cause death." Abraham said: "Surely God causes the Sun to rise in the East, now you cause it to rise in the West.

The verse describes the defeated party:

> Thus was the unbeliever utterly confounded. God guides not such people of wrongdoers (to attain their goals). (Baqara 2:258)

In this way this verse is an example of the struggle against powerful rulers. Other examples could be given. This meeting and others like it most probably happened in public with witnesses.

This verse carries an Abrahamic message: those who pit themselves against the truth will eventually lose.

His Death

Prophet Abraham's death also holds meaningful messages and serves as an example. He had grown old, but he did not want to die because of his great love for conveying his message and his desire to continue to worship and work for his mission. He raised his hands in prayer and pleaded with full sincerity and loyalty:

"Oh my Lord, until I ask to die, please do not take my soul!" But God has His own law: "Every living being will taste death." And so even the friend of the Most Merciful had to taste of it.

But, as God accepted Abraham's prayer, it happened in the way Abraham desired. God convinced him by showing him the inevitable consequences of age, thus, one day, Abraham saw a lonely old man wandering in the quiet places outside the city. He sent the man a donkey and brought him to his home. He prepared a large meal and set it before him. The old man was happy and very grateful.

But the man was living his last days, and his mind was coming and going. He was so disabled that when he tried to bring a bite to his mouth, it went instead to his ears and eyes before he finally managed to locate his mouth. Yet when he got the food into his stomach he was unable to digest it before it exited his body.

Prophet Abraham was shocked to see the man's situation. He asked:

"Why are you thus, my dear guest?" The weak man sighed,

"Oh, old age! Oh, Abraham!" and complained about his aged weakness. Suddenly the Friend of God, remembering his own age, whispered, "How old are you?"

When he answered, Prophet Abraham felt even more distressed, as they were only two years apart. Not wanting to find himself in a similar situation, which he now realized could happen in just two years, he said trembling,

"I am only two years younger than you; will I be like this when I reach your age?"

"Yes, certainly! How can you doubt it?" the old man responded.

With this answer death seemed very desirable to Prophet Abraham and he made supplication to his Beloved Friend:

"Oh my Lord! Take my spirit before I fall into this condition; take me to Your presence!"

His prayer was accepted. The old man changed his shape, and took Prophet Abraham's soul. The decrepit person had actually been the Angel of Death sent with this purpose.[28]

PART TWO

The Virtues of the Prophet Abraham

B efore embarking on a point-by-point discussion of the virtues of the Prophet Abraham, who is held up by the Qur'an as an example to follow and obey, I would like to draw attention to a few points:

1- To make it easier to benefit from the Abrahamic virtues, it is best to divide them into two categories:

a. Those which are attained, the virtues any human being can attain through striving with the will, such as being dutiful, thankful, and merciful.

b. Those which are granted. They cannot be gained through struggle and effort, but are only a gift of God; these are virtues such as being shown the angels, or being the conveyer of Revelation in the form of a Book or Scripture.

2- Some virtues (belonging to both categories) are observed in other prophets, while other virtues were given specifically to Abraham alone. For example, only the Prophet Abraham is called *Halilullah* (Friend of God) in the Qur'an. Some virtues were also given to other prophets; for example, the honor of being greeted by God, extraordinary patience, and perfect purity of intention. Another virtue which is a characteristic of every prophet is specifically emphasized over and over for the Prophet Abraham: that he did not associate partners with God. It is repeated in seven different places that he was not one of those who associated partners with God.

The Qur'an inspires contemplation of the truths hidden in these details by our Almighty Creator; in other words, we should extract and examine the lessons God puts before us in the subtle meanings of these facts.

With this in mind, in explaining the Abrahamic virtues I will not stop at these two categories, but will go into other explanations, comparisons, and reminders, attempting to present some additional information. Also, I will relate some personal interpretations and conclusions which may be of interest.

All of what I will be addressing is simply a few small drops from the ocean of the Qur'an. Everyone, I believe, may be able to discover some new messages in it according to their character, background, interest, and perseverance.

ATTAINED VIRTUES

The virtues in this group are those which perseverance and struggle can attain or develop. It is these virtues that the people who love and follow Abraham are commanded to take as an example. Some Islamic scholars, basing their opinions on the Qur'an, conclude that Abraham's persistent striving in these virtues was the reason he was exalted by God with gifts and privileges, most of all his prophethood. There is great benefit in knowing these Abrahamic virtues: they are within reach for everyone despite our human limitations. Since his prophethood was given him because of his persistence in these virtues, we can see that (though not everyone can be a prophet) every person can gain higher spiritual stations through striving for these virtues.

After first addressing these virtues, I will move on to the second group, God-given virtues. These virtues are precious gifts of the utmost value. Their great value, in turn, is proof of the greatness of Abraham's success in using his free will to pursue them, and of their great importance in the sight of God.

This means that even in prophethood, how one chooses to use free will has a role in determining the progress that can be made.

USING REASON IN MATTERS OF FAITH

The most outstanding aspect of the Prophet Abraham that needs to be mentioned here is his reasoning in issues of faith. Although it is not stated outright in the Qur'an that he used reason to derive all of the six principles of faith, it does mention his reasoning on the issues of (a) the existence of God and of (b) life after death, which are the beginning of all belief. This Qur'anic passage, concerned with the method he used to call his people to faith, describes from a different perspective his use of reason in reaching *tawhid* (faith in the Oneness of God):

– Thus We had showed Abraham (the ugliness and irrationality of polytheism and) the inner dimension of the heavens and the earth, and the eternal truth – this We had done so that he might be one of those who have achieved certainty of faith:

When the night overspread over him, he saw a star; and he exclaimed: "This is my Lord, (is it)?" But when it set (sank from sight), he said: "I love not the things that set."

And when (on another night), he beheld the full moon rising in splendor, he said: "This is my Lord, (is it)!" But when it set, he said: "Unless my Lord guided me, I would surely be among the people gone astray."

– Then, when he beheld the sun rising in all its splendor, he said: "This is my Lord, (is it)? This one is the greatest of all!" But when it set, he said: "O my people! Surely I am free from your association of partners with God and from whatever you associate with Him as partners. have turned my face (my whole being) with pure faith and submission to the One Who has originated the heavens and the earth each with particular features, and I am not one of those associating partners with God." (An'am 6:75-79)

The conclusion of the verse (3:67), *He (Abraham) was never of those who associate partners with God* removes a serious misunderstanding concerning the verses above. Unfortunately, some interpreters of the Qur'an have misunderstood from the Prophet Abraham's mentioning a star, and then the moon, and then the sun, as his Lord, that he took these heavenly objects as Lord for a short time one after the other before being chosen as Prophet. Whereas the verses are explicit about the fact he made a mental and spiritual journeying in the *malakut* (the inner dimension of existence) to have certainty of faith, not faith simply, according to his rank as one near-stationed to God. In addition, He mentioned them as his Lord also to demonstrate to his people that none of the heavenly objects could be the Lord. He openly declared before he beheld the sun and said that it was "his" Lord: "Unless my Lord guided me, I would surely be among the people gone astray." If he had not yet found his true Lord—God Almighty, he would not have said: "Unless my Lord guided me."

If we look at the end of the verse regarding the Prophet Abraham's mental and spiritual journeying, it shows in a more obvious way that his call to his people was a carefully prepared invitation. It is highly possible that this was his first invitation to his people, since the following verse describes the reaction that the people gave: "His people set out to remonstrate with him."

Later, the verses which follow this relate what his people said in other disagreement(s) which may have occurred at different times:

> "Do you remonstrate with me concerning God, when He has guided me (to the right way)? (Do not attempt to threaten me, for) I do not fear those that you associate with Him as partners (and who have no power to give harm or benefit on their behalf); whatever my Lord wills will happen, and no evil will befall me unless He so wills. My Lord embraces all things within His Knowledge. Will you not, then, think, take heed, and come to your senses? Why should I fear those that you associate with God as partners when you do not fear associating partners with Him without His ever having sent down on you any warrant therefore? Think, then, which of the two parties has the right to feel secure?—answer me, if you have anything to do with knowledge." (An'am 6:80:81)

Reflecting on these verses, it is possible to imagine how his people reacted against Abraham in words and actions. For instance, these lines show that the idol worshippers threatened the Prophet Abraham with their idols, saying that the wrath and curses of these gods would be turned on him. The Qur'an also gives the example of the people to whom Prophet Hud came, who threatened him thus: "We say nothing but that some of our deities have possessed you with some evil" (Hud 11:54).

The argument which began thus gradually became more heated, leading to the breaking of the idols, the struggle with Nimrod, the attempted execution, and the emigration.

As clearly mentioned in the Qur'an, Abraham also sought to increase his certainty in faith regarding resurrection from the dead. In a way it was a search related to resurrection in the Hereafter. Since the second most important essential of faith, the belief in life after death, is a concern of each and every person, the Prophet Abraham embarked on a rational search on behalf of all humanity, and made a request of his Sustainer:

> And recall when Abraham said: "My Lord, show me how You will restore life to the dead!" God responded: "Why? Do you not believe?" Abraham replied: "Yes, but in order that my heart be at rest." God ordered: "Then take four birds each of a different kind, and tame them to yourself so that you know them fully. Then cut them into pieces and mix the pieces with each other. Put a piece from each on every hill, and then summon them, and they will come flying to you. Know that surely God is All-Honored (with irresistible might), All-Wise." (Baqara 2:260)

Razi articulates a fundamental principle for unshakeable faith that is presented to humanity by these verses: "This verse shows that faith must be based on proof and evidence, not on imitation." I would like to emphasize that one of the clearest Abrahamic messages is "reason in faith."

Prophet Muhammad, peace and blessings be upon him, in order to emphasize that we have a greater need than Abraham for reason in faith, said to his community, i.e. all Muslims, "We are more subject to doubt than the Prophet Abraham."[1] Scholars have interpreted this saying in many ways. Since they are too many to mention here I will give only one interpretation. Prophet Muhammad (using "we" to refer to himself) must have meant: "As I do not doubt, so too the Prophet Abraham never doubted. For if the prophets were subject to doubt, I would be the first to doubt, but you know that I have never fallen into doubt. Thus you can know that he too never doubted."[2]

But in general, it is accepted that the Prophet Abraham wanted his certainty (*yaqin*) to be increased.[3] There are many levels of certainty. Just three have been comprehended by humans:

a) Certainty coming from knowledge,
b) Certainty coming from observation,
c) Certainty coming from experience.

As in every situation, the main way to increase one's knowledge is through *tahqiq*, searching and investigating. It was the Prophet Abraham who showed the way to this path. In our time, when materialism threatens to replace religion, faith can only be saved by entering the door of investigating that was opened by the Prophet Abraham.

NOT ASSOCIATING PARTNERS WITH GOD

The most unique characteristic of the Prophet Abraham, declared repeatedly in the Qur'an, is his being "not of the *mushrikin* (those who associate partners with God)." This is a very significant expression itself. For it is said of Abraham a total of six times: "Abraham was never of those who associate partners with God."[4] In one place he makes the same statement himself. "I am not of the *mushrikin*,"[5] he says.

Certainly it is clear that a prophet would not fall into this category. Thus the repetition of the statement that the Prophet Abraham was "not of the *mushrikin*" must be intended to show the degree of sensitivity he had toward *tawhid*, the oneness of God. This leads to the following interpretation: As there are degrees of belief and unbelief, so there are degrees of *tawhid*, awareness of God's oneness. The Prophet Abraham was at the peak of this awareness. The other unique characteristics of the Prophet Abraham mentioned in the Qur'an are reflections of this *tawhid*. For example, he went to meet his Creator with a peaceful heart, for his complete and faultless *tawhid* allowed him to do so. Looking at this from the opposite perspective, remembering that the Prophet Abraham is an example, we can say that his moral values led him to true *tawhid* and finally provided him peace in his reunion with the Creator.

It may seem strange to use expressions like "levels of *tawhid*" or "perfected *tawhid*" according to the fundamental view of Imam Maturidi: "Faith is undivided; it does not increase or decrease." Without getting into this theological discussion I want to mention one or two points which will explain the concept.

God Almighty says in chapter Yusuf (Joseph), verse 106, "And most of them do not even believe in God without associating partners with Him." This verse declares that some people, while believing in God as the creator of the universe, also have some incorrect assumptions about Him.[6]

The hadith regarding lesser *shirk* (associating partners with God) warn that not only Christians, Jews, or Arabs of the pre-Islamic era, but even devout Muslims, can fall into *shirk* while believing in God without realizing it. In one of his sayings related in *al-Mustadrak*, Prophet Muhammad sets a measure which should be meditated on seriously: Love. The love which is cultivated in one's heart determines one's religion. If this is not centered on God, it is a type of *shirk*. In order to be able to escape *shirk*, one must consciously control the spirituality of the heart and all the emotions of the heart such as love, hate, approval, reproof, and resentment, directing them toward the goal of pleasing God. Before relating the hadith, this is a perfect place to refer to the late Said Nursi's apposite statement about compassion. According to him, love and compassion—which the hadith puts at the center of faith and *tawhid*—form the core of the character, while intense feelings that originate from compassion (in other words, every type of human feeling) represent different manifestations of it: "A believing human being's... various intense emotions are transformations of that capacity to love God, and distillations of it in other forms."[7]

The standard set by the Pride of the Worlds, Prophet Muhammad, was: "*Shirk* is more hidden than the sound of a tiny ant's footsteps walking on the hill of Safa on a dark night. The smallest degree of this *shirk* is to love despite oppression, injustice, or to dislike despite justice." God Almighty has commanded, "If you love God, obey me!"[8] Also, in the first verse of Sura al-Mumtahana it is stated that those who love the enemies of God will go astray from the straight path due to this love.

In order to clarify this concept, I would like to note that in the sayings of the Prophet those who excessively love money are described as *abd al-dinar* (servants of money), and those who excessively love clothing are described as *abd al-qadifa* (servants of clothing); those described thus are reproved.[9] Besides this, many beliefs and actions are defined as *shirk*, such as hypocrisy,[10] swearing oaths based on pre-Islamic (idolatrous) traditions,[11] belief in bad luck,[12] and casting spells.[13]

The Abrahamic *tawhid*, belief in the absolute unity of God, which the Qur'an lauds and repeatedly presents to the attention of Muslims is a *tawhid* which is free of even the smallest and subtlest form of *shirk*. The late Razi describes the Prophet Abraham's *tawhid*: "Those who are familiar with Qur'anic science know that the Prophet Abraham, so to speak, swam in an ocean of *tawhid*."[14]

And this ideal is presented to believers as the ultimate dream and goal, since we are told that in the Prophet Abraham we have the best of examples.[15]

SUBMITTING TO GOD

One of the most important messages the Prophet Abraham brought is submission to God. Long before Prophet Muhammad, it was the Prophet Abraham who brought the religion of Islam to humanity, the religion of the purest *tawhid* on Earth today; it was he who first called its followers "Muslims" (meaning those who are submitted to God). This is stated in a Qur'anic verse: *God named you Muslims previously...* (Hajj 22:78).

However much the word *muslim* has come to refer to "one who accepts the religion conveyed by Prophet Muhammad," the dictionary meaning of the Arabic word is "one who obeys and submits to God." In other words, it means a person who has sincerely submitted whole-heartedly to God and His path. I am of the opinion that this terminology enables a thoughtful understanding of the spirit of Islam and its fundamental purpose. In a religion which is free from all human (fallible) concepts and completely based on revelation from God Almighty, "complete submission" is a highly important prerequisite. One either accepts or rejects the concept of God's revelation and its being above what is human. After acceptance, complete submission is the only way to approach matters regarding the Unseen which are beyond human power. Hence, it is mentioned in the Qur'an "When God and His Messenger have decreed a matter, it is not for a believing man and a believing woman to have an option in any of the matters concerning them,"(Ahzab 33:36) and in another verse, ". . . they will not truly believe until they make you the judge regarding any dispute between them, and then they will not find the least vexation within themselves over what you have decided, and they will surrender in full submission" (Nisa 4:65).

We can also see in the Qur'an another example of the relation between Islam and the Prophet Abraham. God Almighty urges him to submit, and he immediately accepts.

> When his Lord told him, "Submit yourself wholly (to your Lord)," he responded: "I have submitted myself wholly to the Lord the Worlds." (Baqara 2:131)

Razi mentions that the majority of scholars agree on the fact that the command "Submit!" came to the Prophet Abraham before his prophethood, even before he reached puberty, when he was seeking the truth about the existence of God Almighty through questioning the nature and authority of the sun and the moon. He gives this evidence: "This command does not mean, 'Become a Muslim!' (meaning a follower of the religion of Islam.) Instead it means: 'Obey the limitations set by My Revelation, and the laws of Creation; embrace

My commands with enthusiasm! Stay away from rebellion of the heart and of the tongue, fulfill your obligations and worship sincerely and solely for My sake, and do not fall into the falsehood of associating partners with Me.'"[16]

It is very thought-provoking that this command "submit" has such a unique grammatical style that there is no room for doubt about its meaning. Expanding on Razi's thoughts, I will attempt to relate different perspectives on the nature of the command "submit" for those who would like to pursue the honor of following the Prophet Abraham:

- Submission to commands that please one as well as those which do not,
- that relate to this world as well as to the Hereafter,
- that fit the style of our era as well as those which do not,
- that are appreciated by others as well as those which are condemned,
- give us personal, familial or, national benefits as well as those which do not,

Submit to every command from the Word of God!

Prophet Muhammad, who restored the religion of the Prophet Abraham, extended the concept of submission, which was offered by God Almighty to the Prophet Abraham by asking his followers to submit both in ease and in difficulty, in times of joy and times of sadness; to submit with no objections, obeying the rules and regulations of the religion, meanwhile ignoring all criticism and even obeying the ruling authority as long as there was no explicit persecution.[17]

In order to understand the degree of the Prophet Abraham's submission to the orders of God it is enough to remember his one-man struggle against the people of Nimrod and his breaking of the idols, which was enough to cause the people to attack him mercilessly, and the fact that he showed no signs of doubt or fear when thrown into the fire.

TRUTHFULNESS

If faith and submission are the first characteristics of a person's growth, it can be said that truthfulness is not far behind. In the same way, the saintly Abu Bakr was second only to Prophet Muhammad in truthfulness, the most well known of his virtuous characteristics. The Qur'an mentions truthfulness as one of the Prophet Abraham's most renowned characteristics:

> And make mention of Abraham in the Book. He was surely a
> sincere man of truth, a Prophet. (Mary 19:41)

A question may arise when we remember that on the Day of Judgment the Prophet Abraham has this excuse for those who come to him asking for supplication on their behalf, "I have lied three times; I can make no intercession before God."[18] They were not actual lies; otherwise it would not be compatible with the trustworthiness of any Prophet, let alone the "intimate friend of God." The Messenger of God, after stating that Prophet Abraham never lied in his life, explains the 3 "lies" mentioned above in the following hadith:

> Twice for the sake of God when he said, "Indeed I am sick," and
> he said, "Rather (some doer) must have done it—this is the
> biggest of them." The (third was) that while Abraham and Sarah
> (his wife) were going (on a journey) they passed by (the territo-
> ry of) a tyrant. Someone said to the tyrant, "This man (i.e.
> Abraham) is accompanied by a very charming lady." So, he sent
> for Abraham and asked him about Sarah saying, "Who is this
> lady?" Abraham said, "She is my sister." Abraham went to Sarah
> and said, "O Sarah! There are no believers on the surface of the
> earth except you and I. This man asked me about you and I have
> told him that you are my sister, so don't contradict my statement."
> The tyrant then called Sarah and when she went to him, he tried
> to take hold of her with his hand, but (his hand got stiff and) he
> was confounded. He asked Sarah. "Pray to God for me, and I
> shall not harm you." So Sarah asked God to cure him and he got
> cured. He tried to take hold of her for the second time, but (his
> hand got as stiff as or stiffer than before and) was more confound-
> ed. He again requested Sarah, "Pray to God for me, and I will not

harm you." Sarah asked God again and he became alright. He then called one of his guards (who had brought her) and said, "You have not brought me a human being but have brought me a devil." The tyrant then gave Hajar as a girl-servant to Sarah. Sarah came back (to Abraham) while he was praying. Abraham, gesturing with his hand, asked, "What has happened?" She replied, "God has spoiled the evil plot of the infidel (or immoral person) and gave me Hagar for service."[19]

There is a completely unique message here about how Prophet Abraham's followers should react to lying; his extreme embarrassment before God because of these "ambiguous words," one of which was part of the strategy to eliminate associating partners with God, and thus was actually spoken against the world of lies and all untruth, while the other was spoken to save his life from a tyrant. In my opinion his truthfulness is confirmed by God in the following verse none of what he said was a lie: *He was surely a sincere man of truth, a Prophet* (Mary 19:41). By referring to the Abraham's word "I have lied three times; I can make no intercession before God,"[20], Prophet Muhammad in order to make it clear in the mind of believers how evil lies are—this was a stylistic device to get across this message: "Our leader and example Prophet Abraham felt this much regret and shame before God for having said even once in his life something ambiguous (not even an actual lie) to escape from danger...." Likewise some scholars hold that "such words which may come to have two senses are not absolute lies," and go on to give extended explanations of Prophet Abraham's words. For example, the word for "I am sick" in the Arabic language, can also have the meaning "I am going to be sick," in addition to the immediate meaning "at this moment I am sick, and thus Prophet Abraham may have meant that he was going to be unwell. They also comment that he only said "Rather (some doer) must have done it—this is the biggest of them" to underline the ridiculousness of the people's belief that the idols have the power to bless or harm; this statement, thus, was intended to direct them to the logical conclusion that if they understood the ridiculousness of the idols destroying one another, then they should understand that "idols are not God."[21] Yazır also says of Prophet Abraham's statement "I am sick": "Since they had invited him to worship with them, and as they were astrologists, he looked at the stars as if he were weighing this, appearing as if he were checking the positions of the stars; then he said 'I am not feeling well,' giving a reason for declining the invitation."[22]

HANIF (LENIENT AND TOLERANT)

One word which comes immediately to mind when thinking of the Prophet Abraham is *hanif*. This word is found 10 times in the Qur'an. Almost each time this word is used it refers to the Prophet Abraham; most of the time it refers directly, while the others are indirect references. There are five references to "the *hanif* religion of Abraham."

The word *hanif* comes from the root *hanaf*. *Hanaf* means going from deviance to soundness, from crookedness to straightness, from misguidance to truth. Thus, one who is *hanif* is one who abandons deviance for the straight path, tending toward right and truth. This word was traditionally used to refer to the religion of the Prophet Abraham even during the Age of Ignorance before the advent of Islam.[23] It refers to those who "turn from false idols and religions, and surrender only to the one God."

According to the explanations given in the hadith, being *hanif* is not only abandoning deviation for truth, but at the same time means practicing lenience, tolerance and simplicity. The Prophet said, as we saw earlier, "I was sent with the lenient, tolerant and easy religion of the *hanif*." He made this statement at explaining that Muslims could participate in acceptable festival entertainments (if there isn't anything God has forbidden). At one time his wife Aisha clarified that the Messenger of God said this so that Jews would know that there is tolerance in Islam. According to another report, she said that he made the explanation "Jews and Christians should know that our religion is inclusive."[24]

Confirming that the *hanif* religion includes lenience, tolerance, and simplicity as fundamental principles, the Prophet also made this explanation:

"The most pleasing religion before God Almighty is the tolerant religion of the *hanif* (worshipping the one God)."[25] "The most beneficial path you can follow is the easiest."[26] The Qur'an states that the *hanif* religion of Abraham is essentially built on ease, lenience, and tolerance:

> . . . (God) has not laid any hardship on you in religion. This is the way of your father Abraham. (Hajj 22:78)

This kind of tolerance and lenience taken from the religion of Abraham became one of the fundamental principles of the Prophet's teaching method:

> (O Messenger,) it was by a mercy from God that, (at the time of the reversal,) you were lenient with them (your Companions). Had you been harsh and hard-hearted, they would surely have scattered away from about you. (Al Imran 3:159)

Aisha, mother of believers, reported that God's Messenger always preferred the least strenuous of requirements when he required something of his followers.[27] In addition, he warned people given to extremes who, with an unhealthy motivation to be "the most perfect," remain unsatisfied with perfection and seek hardship and difficulties: "The religion of Islam is a moderate way. Whoever seeks to best others by competing in religion will be bested by religion (and cannot be successful). Thus you should take the middle way, do your best according to your strength and capacity, and always give good news…"[28]

Therefore, lenience and tolerance are fundamental Abrahamic messages.

BEING PATIENT AND GOD-CONSCIOUS

One of the most unique characteristics of the Prophet Abraham is his patience. Many of the trials and tribulations that the Prophet Abraham successfully passed through that are described in the Qur'an were tests requiring patience, fortitude, gravity, and firm belief—total submission to God Almighty—tests such as imprisonment, being thrown into the fire, being expelled from his country (emigration), having to leave his family in the desert, and being asked to sacrifice his son. He showed a highly mature level of patience through all of them.

His patience was a natural consequence of his faith and submission to God Almighty. These also allowed him to serve and worship his Sustainer faultlessly. He was extremely sensitive in performing the ritual acts of worship and remembrance of God. Prophet Muhammad explains how he got the title *Halilullah* (Friend of God) by relating a prayer which he prayed each morning and night:

> So, after all, declare God's being absolutely free of any defects and exalted above having any partners when you enter the evening and when you enter the morning; and due to Him is all the praise in the heavens and on the earth—and in the late afternoon and when you enter the noon time. (Rum 30:17-18)

Tabari mentions that the Prophet Abraham received the honor of becoming a Friend of God due to his firmness of character in two things: patience and devoted servanthood to God.[29] He even draws attention to the point that all other blessings on the Prophet Abraham were due to these same two features of his character, blessings such as "being the leader and example to all people coming after him, being a Prophet to his people and having more prophets—even those entrusted with Scriptures—coming from his bloodline. When one of these important and reputable descendents died, another blessed one was sent in their place. He came to be loved by all nations. Today, everyone remembers and eulogizes him."[30]

There is more evidence for the importance of these two characteristics which led Abraham to be blessed with the "friendship" of God in the story of Prophet Joseph as related in the Qur'an. Chapter Yusuf describes Prophet Joseph's journey from the bottom of the well, after being sold in the market as a slave, to becoming Egypt's high minister of finance, and Joseph himself tells his awe-stricken brothers that these two unique characteristics—patience and piety—brought him there:

> "I am Joseph, and this is my brother. God has indeed been gracious to us. Truly, whoever keeps from disobedience to God in piety and reverence for Him and is patient, it is certain that God will not leave to waste the reward of those devoted to doing good consciously so that God sees them." (Yusuf 12:90)

It is useful to clarify that this "patience" and "piety" (*taqwa*), two great characteristics that open the doors of both the material and spiritual worlds, are not a birthright, but rather are developed over time by persistent striving. The Prophet Abraham taught these two as part of his message to the believers, and gave them as a Godly gift to the fortunate people determined to follow his way; they can open many doors which are closed to ignorant people.

Finally I would like to mention that even though "patience" and "piety" are essentially two different characteristics, I refer to them together because they are generally referred to together in the Qur'an. In fact neither one of these can really exist without the other. How can piety be possible without patience, and how can continual patience be satisfactorily maintained without piety? In a hadith of the Prophet Muhammad, he is quoted as saying that true patience, which will lift the human spirit to new heights, is manifested in three situations: "Patience against trials and tribulations, patience in continuous worship, and patience in avoiding (the committing of) sins."[31]

All three of these grow from "piety"; likewise, without them there is no real piety.

GRATEFULNESS FOR GOD'S BLESSINGS

Gratefulness is one of the fundamental and requisite elements of true servanthood in a believer's relationship with God. In other words, it is recognizing that all the blessings and temporal possessions we receive are given by God Almighty. In a sense, we are swimming in an ocean of countless favors, although we are aware of few of them.

Existence itself, life, being human, the gift of faith, belief in the Oneness of God and belonging to the community of Prophet Muhammad, being healthy, etc., are each precious blessings in their own right. We are unable to show sufficient gratitude for the greatness of even one of them, and most of the time we do not recognize these as blessings. Going into the different material and spiritual blessings each individual receives would require more space than we have here.

It is necessary that a person, knowing that all of these blessings are from our Sustainer, be full of gratitude each moment before the Creator. Because gratitude and praise must be the foundation of a believer's relationship with God, the Qur'an begins with praise; likewise Muslims' most important act of worship, the five daily prayers, begin with praise, continue with praise, and conclude with 33 repetitions of remembrance of God in praise. The meaning of the beautiful word *Alhamdulillah* also shows how essential it is to praise God: "God is the rightful recipient of absolutely all praise and thanks, whoever may utter it, and whomever it is directed to, from the beginning of time until eternity, God—the Existent without whom nothing can exist."[32]

The Prophet Abraham had the honor of becoming an example to the people who follow him by fulfilling this important act of worship (praising God) to the utmost degree. Whenever we mention him and his message, praising God and being grateful to God should come immediately to mind. A Qur'anic verse explains:

> Abraham was an exemplary leader, (whose self-dedication to the good of his community made him) as if a community, sincerely obedient to God as a man of pure faith (free from any stain of unbelief and hypocrisy), and he was not of those who associate partners with God. Always thankful for His favors. (Nahl 16:120-121)

CLEANLINESS

Keeping the Masjid al-Haram (The Inviolable House of Worship) clean for hajj pilgrims is mentioned in the Qur'an as one of the important duties given to the Prophet Abraham.[33] Previously I mentioned that he not only took care of the Ka'ba, but declared its surroundings and all of Mecca a sacred precinct. Based on this policy I suggest that he could be called "the first environmentalist" or "the master environmentalist." However, these titles are still insufficient to give an idea of his approach to the issue of cleanliness, which is far broader and far more inclusive than simply caring about the environment. In a hadith, the Prophet Muhammad, peace be upon him, mentions that many hygienic practices of everyday life that differentiate human beings from other creatures were introduced to humanity by the Prophet Abraham. As will be seen more clearly in the section "Father of Firsts," many of the practices he initiated were related to bodily cleanliness.

Relating all these actions to the Prophet Abraham honors him on the one hand, while on the other it draws attention to their importance throughout the ages—like all Abrahamic messages—for human life.

DEVOTION IN CARRYING OUT HIS CHARGE

Another characteristic of the Prophet Abraham was his complete and conscientious fulfillment of the duty and charges given to him. He is mentioned in the Qur'an as *Abraham who perfectly fulfilled whatever was due to him* (Najm 53:37). Said Ibn Jubayr and Sawri write about the Prophet Abraham's perfect completion of the tasks given him by God.[34] In the above verse God Almighty speaks thus of Abraham, among other things for his devotion to teaching the Oneness of God, an act for which he took the risk of being thrown into the fire. In fact, his life was full of trials and special missions and he gained his reputation by fulfilling every one of these with the same conscientiousness described in the verse. In the same way scholars[35] have pointed out that the verse also refers to other duties, such as being a leader to his people, constructing and maintaining the Ka'ba, and others which are listed in the following verse:

(So) remember that his Lord tested Abraham with severe commandments and terrible ordeals (such as being thrown into a fire, the destruction of the people of Lot, his relatives, and being ordered to sacrifice his son Ishmael), and that he fulfilled them thoroughly." (Baqara 2:124)

Nevertheless, the Prophet Abraham showed his faithful desire to gain the pleasure of God Almighty through all his trials and tribulations, whether it was being told in his dream to sacrifice his son, reasoning about the heavenly bodies, breaking the idols, or leaving his people.[36] According to Ibn Abbas' explanation, the things the Prophet Abraham fulfilled faultlessly include ten mandatory rituals in his religion, which became *sunna* acts in Islam, or traditions of Prophet Muhammad that are recommended for his followers: "cleaning the mouth and nose, having haircuts, trimming the mustache, brushing the teeth, circumcision, shaving the armpits, cutting the nails, and washing the private parts after using the bathroom."[37] A hadith calls these "ten things befitting human nature."[38]

Some scholars say that the number of commands with which the Prophet Abraham was tested was thirty.[39] These thirty orders reflect the virtues listed in four different chapters of the Qur'an:

- Ten are mentioned in chapter Ahzab:

> Surely all men and women who submit to God, and all truly believing men and truly believing women, and all devoutly obedient men and devoutly obedient women, and all men and women honest and truthful in their speech, and all men and women who persevere, and all men and women humble, and all men and women who give in alms, and all men and women who fast, and all men and women who guard their chastity (and avoid exposing their private parts), and all men and women who remember and mention God much—for them God has prepared forgiveness and a tremendous reward. (Ahzab 33:35)

- Ten are mentioned in chapter Tawba:

> Those who constantly return to God in repentance, and those who are devoted to worshipping God, and those who live in praise of God, and those who travel, and those who bow down

to God in adoration, and those who prostrate themselves before God in submission, and those who enjoin and promote what is right and good and who forbid and try to prevent evil, and those who keep to the bounds set by God: give glad tidings to such believers. (Tawba 9:112)

- Ten are found in chapter Mu'minun:

Prosperous indeed are the believers. They are in their Prayer humble and fully submissive, overwhelmed by awe, the grandeur and majesty of God. They always turn away from and avoid whatever is vain and frivolous. They are constantly engaged in the purification of their own selves and wealth, as well as in the task of purifying others (in a constant effort to give the Prescribed Purifying Alms).They strictly guard their private parts, and their chastity and modesty, save from their spouses or, those whom they rightfully possess, for with regard to them they are free from blame. But whoever seeks beyond that, such are truly transgressors. They are faithfully true to their trusts and to their pledges. They safeguard all their Prayers including all the rituals of which the Prayer is composed. Those illustrious ones are the inheritors, who will inherit the highest level of Paradise. Therein they will abide for ever. (Mu'minun 23:1-11)

- Ten of them are mentioned in chapter Ma'arij:

Not so, however, those who regularly perform the Prayer. Those who are constant at their Prayer, and those in whose wealth there is a portion acknowledged (by them), for the needy with no means other than begging and who are denied (help because they cannot beg and are thought to be well-off), those who confirm the Day of Judgment, and those who are fearful of their Lord's punishment and live accordingly. Behold, their Lord's punishment is that of which no one can ever feel secure. And those who strictly guard their private parts, and their chastity and modesty, save from their spouses or, those whom they rightfully possess, for with regard to them they are free from blame. But whoever seeks beyond that, such are truly transgressors; those who are faithfully true to their trusts, and to their pledges, and those who are upholders (of right and justice) by bearing true witness and without avoiding giving testimony, and those who safeguard all their Prayers, including all the rituals of which a

Prayer is composed. Those will be in Gardens, highly-honored. (Ma'arij 70:22-35)

Ibn Abbas said, "No one else but the Prophet Abraham has been tested with all these and managed to fulfill them all."[40] Although some scholars have said that the commands or tests were thirty in number, Ibn Abbas' narration lists the above four passages of the Qur'an which each contain ten, and thus states that the Prophet Abraham was tested with forty virtues of Islam.[41] However, a closer look shows that some are repeated, and if we count these only once, the total comes to thirty.

In order to show that varying views about the trials of the Prophet Abraham have been adopted by different Muslim scholars it is worthwhile to point out that some put the number at ten; six of these are related to care of the human body, and four are related to the hajj. Those related to the person are shaving the axillary and pubic hair, circumcision, trimming the nails and mustache, and making full ablution (bath) before Friday prayer, while those related to the pilgrimage are circumambulating the Ka'ba, running between the hills of Safa and Marwa, stoning a pillar that symbolizes Satan, and traveling from Arafat to Muzdalifa.[42]

In summary, taking seriously any duty that falls to us and completing it in the most beautiful way by putting forward our best effort is one of the messages presented to us by Abraham's life. People who would like to gain the pleasure of God Almighty through the path of the Prophet Abraham should keep this in mind.

HOSPITALITY

One of the most well-known virtues of the Prophet Abraham was his hospitality. It is narrated that he was known as the first person to host guests and called "the father of guests."[43] In the Qur'an it is stated that he slaughtered a fatted calf and prepared a meal for unexpected, unknown guests who had not even made their need (hunger) explicit.[44] One may ask "how do we know that the Prophet Abraham did not know these people?" The fact that the travelers refused to eat the food shows that it was prepared without their requesting it, and similarly, the Prophet Abraham's unease when they didn't reach for the food shows that they were strangers. Slaughtering a fatted calf and preparing a beautiful dinner for guests whom he did not know and was not expecting is Qur'anic evidence of the Prophet Abraham's high degree of generosity and hospitality.

Preparing meals for guests, be they stranger or friend, is thus an Abrahamic message regarding social interaction.

STRENGTH IN WORSHIP AND INTELLIGENCE IN RELIGION

According to the Qur'an, another aspect of the Prophet Abraham is that he was among the strong and intelligent:

> And remember Our servants Abraham and Isaac and Jacob, all of them endowed with power (in obedience to God and doing good deeds), and sound insight (to be able to discern the truth in all things and events). We made them perfectly pure and sincere in their devotion so that they were wholly bent on the Abode of the Hereafter in their thoughts, speeches, and acts. Most certainly, they are in Our sight among the perfectly purified, chosen, the truly good![45]

The commentators have interpreted the words *ulu'l-yad* in the verse to mean "power." They explain that the Prophet Abraham was intelligent since he spent all his material power on works related to faith and the Hereafter. He was purely directed toward gaining God's pleasure, without the least inclination toward worldly pleasure for its own sake.[46]

And what else could really be expected from the Prophet Abraham, who is said to have reached absolute *tawhid*, but this; being completely faithful, completely oriented toward God and the life to come, and completely devoted to worship! Intelligence in religion is to know God Almighty, see Him in every blessing, seek our sustenance only from Him, and work for the Hereafter.

If we wonder about the secret of the intelligence, sincerity, and *tawhid* of Abraham, we find the answer in his understanding of God and life. He spoke of this understanding in his explanation to his idol-worshipping people:

> I see that they (all that you worship) are enemies to me, but the Lord of the worlds is not.
>
> He Who has created me and so guides me (to whatever is to my benefit in both this world and the next). And He it is Who gives me food and drink. And Who, when I fall ill, heals me. And Who will make me die and then will bring me back to life. And Who, I hope, will forgive me my faults on Judgment Day.
>
> My Lord! Grant me true, wise judgment, and join me with the righteous.
>
> And grant me a most true and virtuous renown among posterity. And make me one of the inheritors of the Garden abounding in bounties and blessings. And forgive my father, for he is among those who have gone astray. And do not disgrace me on the Day when all people will be raised up to life. The Day when neither wealth will be of any use, nor offspring, but only he (will prosper) who comes before God with a sound heart (free of all kinds of unbelief, hypocrisy, and associating partners with God). (Shuara 26:77-89)

Likewise, the Prophet Abraham knew all that he had achieved and succeeded at in life were from God, and thus set the best example of how to reach true *tawhid*, belief in one and only God without associating any partners.

CLEMENT, TENDER-HEARTED, AND EVER-TURNING TO GOD WITH ALL HIS HEART

A Qur'anic verse mentions together three virtues of the Prophet Abraham:

> Abraham was indeed most clement, tender-hearted, ever-turning to God with all his heart. (Hud 11:75)

Halim means "clement," one who is sober, even-tempered, calm, and able to endure difficulties. This is a praiseworthy virtue mentioned in the Qur'an 15 times, 12 of which describe God. In one verse this attribute is applied to Prophet Ishmael: translated as *So We gave him the glad tiding of a boy (to grow as one), mild and forbearing* (Saffat 37:101). In another verse it is also attributed to Prophet Jethro (Shu'ayb) (Hud 11:87), and in two separate places it is written that the Prophet Abraham was *halim* (clement) (e.g. Tawba 9:114). Thus, in the Qur'an, gentleness is a unique characteristic of prophets, especially the Prophet Abraham. Baydawi mentions that, since gentleness of character is unique, God Almighty uses *halim* to describe only the Prophet Abraham and the Prophet Ishmael.[47]

Awwah means someone who is aware of their faults and, regretting them deeply, prays with pure and sincere intentions; such a person also has a merciful and soft heart. In the Qur'an it is mentioned in two verses that the Prophet Abraham was *awwah* (usually translated as 'tender-hearted'), and this word is not used to describe any other person. According to Prophetic teaching related by Ibn Hajar, a person who is "*awwah*" is "one who prays continuously to God with full consciousness and respect."[48] Again, Ibn Hajar narrates that according to the previous scholars, "*awwah*" refers to a person who "is gracious," "is deep and knowledgeable in faith," "repents in secret for their secret sins," and "remembers God Almighty."

Munib means a person who seeks refuge in God. It is a virtue extolled in the Qur'an seven times, but only one of these mentions that it was a unique attribute of the Prophet Abraham. He was exceptionally sensitive in realizing his mistakes and sins and turning to God, seeking refuge in His forgiveness. This is yet another Abrahamic virtue that is truly an outstanding example. His success in all the many difficult tests and trials he underwent, which no other person has been destined to face, allowed him to gain the pleasure of his Sustainer without falling into pride or arrogance by seeking refuge in the forgiveness of God—these are important Abrahamic messages.

A HEART FREE OF EVIL

Another virtue of the Prophet Abraham is that his heart was free of evil. One verse says, *He had believed in his Lord with a heart sound and pure (from any trace of insincerity of belief)* (Saffat 37:84). A heart which is free of evil is completely pure, with no spot of fault, sin, doubt, or *shirk*; it is full of love for God and completely submitted to God.[49] A heart clean and free from all evil and faults is the natural result of finding true faith in God and reaching the level of *tawhid* possessed by Abraham, as explained previously. This is not bestowed upon a person, but instead is a result of persistent effort, and thus, is a door which is open to anyone willing to go through trials and prove themselves strong enough to face them, like Abraham. If this were a gift peculiar to Abraham, the "door" by which a clean heart can be reached would have been closed to others, and thus would not have the same meaning as an Abrahamic message.

MERCIFULNESS

One of the virtues of the Prophet Abraham mentioned in the Qur'an is his mercifulness. In fact, his name means "merciful": "Abraham," means "tender, compassionate father" in the original Aramaic. It came to be used as a word for "very merciful."[50]

Before moving on to the main concept it is necessary to clarify a point: according to some traditions, during the Prophet Abraham's spiritual ascension to heaven, he saw some souls who had committed adultery and he prayed for their ruin as he passed by. When he had thus prayed regarding three souls (or seven according to some), God Almighty intervened: "O Abraham! Do not be hasty! (For) you are one whose prayers are accepted. I treat my servants in one of three ways: either they repent and I forgive them, or I raise up righteous generations from their descendants, or they continue in their evil and I punish them."[51]

If we accept the authenticity of this narration, it can be said that the Prophet Abraham, after receiving this divine warning, returned from his ascension with an exemplary mercifulness; in other words, just as Prophet Muhammad's Ascension (Miraj) perfected him in faith, the Prophet Abraham's ascension perfected him in mercy.

Despite his becoming foremost in mercy through this lesson, and his being full of tender and merciful feelings for his father and his people, not only was the Prophet Abraham unsuccessful in winning their loyalty, but he was imprisoned,[52] thrown into the fire,[53] and sent into exile.[54] Through all of this his mercy in word and deed never lessened, such that Prophet Muhammad described his manner toward his people as "sweeter than honey."[55] He never asked God to punish them, saying instead: "My Lord! They have indeed intrigued to cause many among humankind go astray. So, he who follows me is truly of me; while he who disobeys me, surely You are All-Forgiving, All-Compassionate."[56]

The sharpest thing he said to them when they were about to throw him into the fire was:

> "Shame on you and on all that you worship instead of God!
> Will you not reason and understand?"

On the other hand, some prophets, when their people persistently rejected and struggled against them, prayed for their punishment. For example, Prophet Noah said:

> "My Lord! Do not leave on the Earth any from among the unbelievers who will dwell thereon! If You do leave them, they will lead astray Your servants, and they will beget none but shameless, dissolute, extremely ungrateful unbelievers." (Nuh 71:26-27)

Another example is Prophet Moses' prayer regarding the people of the Pharaoh:

> "Our Lord! Surely You have granted Pharaoh and his chiefs splendor and riches in the present worldly life: our Lord, is this that they may lead people astray from Your way?! Our Lord! Destroy their riches, and press upon their hearts, for surely they will not believe until they see a painful punishment." (Yunus 10:88)

The Prophet Abraham's deepest compassion was for his relatives and followers—the members of his community. The prayer which will be repeated most often by the followers of Prophet

Muhammad until the end of time (because it is included in the daily ritual prayers) is a prayer of the Prophet Abraham related in the Qur'an, which asks for God's mercy on all believers. This is no coincidence: it is strong evidence of the compassion of Abraham for those who believe. This prayer is:

> "Our Lord! Forgive me, and my parents, and all the believers, on the Day on which when the Reckoning will be established." (Ibrahim 14:41)

Proudly following Abraham's religion, the Prophet Muhammad told those who urged him to curse the polytheists opposing him, "I was sent as a mercy, not as one who curses,"[57] despite being persecuted unimaginably by these people. He would not even curse those who treated him the worst, saying "O my Sustainer! Forgive my people, for they do not know You," and "from among their descendants there may arise worshippers of God."[58] He never gave way to vengeful thoughts proving he was "sent as a mercy to the worlds,"[59] or in the words of The Angel of the Mountains (Malak al-Jibal): "You (Muhammad) are just as God describes you, merciful and gracious."[60]

Truly the compassion of God's Messenger Muhammad extended beyond just the Muslims: "Whoever persecutes a *dhimmi*[61] becomes my enemy, and whoever is my enemy, I will settle my score with him on the Last Day!"[62] Similar hadiths even tell us that all living things must be treated well, showing the Prophet's compassion and mercy toward "all that draws breath."[63] Thus it is apparent that he was "a mercy to the worlds,"[64] and it can be said that only with this mercy can one follow the path of the Prophet Abraham.

Indeed it was the Prophet Abraham who brought Islam—not only *tawhid,* but all its aspects, while it was Prophet Muhammad who completed and perfected it.

The Inclusiveness of the Prophet Abraham's Compassion

The Qur'an tells us both directly and indirectly that the Prophet Abraham developed a very high degree of mercy. For example, in the two verses mentioned above, it explains that he was *halim* and *awwah* ("compassionate"; see previous discussion). One of these follows a verse that forbids asking forgiveness for those whose condemnation is certain, even if they be relatives; the verse in question then goes on to explain that this command was given because of the Prophet Abraham's prayers for his father to be forgiven. "The prayer of Abraham for the forgiveness of his father was only because of a promise which he had made to him. But when it became clear that he was an enemy of God, Abraham dissociated himself from him. Abraham was most tender-hearted, most clement.[65] His deep compassion is also mentioned in the following verse:

> So when the apprehension left Abraham and the glad tiding was conveyed to him, he began to argue with Our envoys to plead with Us on behalf of the people of Lot. Abraham was indeed most clement, tender-hearted, ever-turning to God with all his heart. (Hud 11:74-75)

Here it is not very clear what Abraham asked for. But a different verse on the same issue clarifies that he pleaded with the angels assigned to destroy Lot's people, saying "But Lot is among them," in hopes this would change their mission. Yet the response of the angels suggests that he did not plead with the motivation solely of saving Lot, but actually wanted to save Lot's people from destruction. God's envoys replied:

> O Abraham! Cease from this! For sure, the command of your Lord has already gone forth; and there is coming upon them a punishment not to be turned back. (Hud 11:76)

As I wish to emphasize once again the way this shows Abraham's ethic of questioning it would be useful to repeat this before leaving the topic of his pleading and its importance: it is almost certain from this explanation of the angels that the Prophet Abraham did not plead thinking only of the Prophet Lot, but rather wanted to save the whole community from destruction, compelled by his high degree of mercy and compassion. Another verse says that his reminding of Lot was an excuse to stay the hand of the angels of destruction. Although the angels told him,

> "We know fully well who is there; we will certainly save him and his family (by allowing them to leave the city), except his wife. It has already been decreed that she will be among those who will stay behind to be destroyed." (Ankabut 29:32)

The Prophet Abraham kept pleading so that the angels—in chapter Hud, the verse cited fully above—had to use a slightly harsher style, "O Abraham! Desist from (pleading to save Lot's people)!..."

Here, through Abraham, a hero of mercy, God Almighty conveys the message that no one can ever go beyond God's mercy; at the same time He shows the boundaries of acceptable behavior and manners in debate.

This episode in the Prophet Abraham's life shows that it is legitimate and ethical in a debate for one side to question the wisdom of a decision if they avoid insincerity and self-seeking (as the Prophet Abraham did) and that the decision- maker may then reply in a more firm manner. It also shows that it is wrong to show compassion or pardon to those God has judged, as some contemporary believers who are not in complete submission to God attempt to do. Among the many types of human errors, the Qur'an points out to the error of praying for the forgiveness of someone who knowingly rejects and opposes God—even if it be someone as close as one's own father. This is another thought-provoking Abrahamic message.

Universal Benevolence

Another of the universal messages of the Prophet Abraham was his treating every person with the best moral behavior. Without discriminating between believer and unbeliever, the obedient and the rebellious, the sinner and the sincere, the good and the bad, he was just to everyone and never violated their rights. As he was the "Friend of God," the honorable spiritual station he represented necessitated this kind of behavior. We can explain this as follows:

In a hadith, the Prophet Muhammad said "A person follows the religion of their (close) friend."[66] In accordance with this prophetic saying, the Prophet Abraham followed the lifestyle and morality that his Friend (God) loves. This lifestyle is universal benevolence—to avoid depriving anyone of their rights and blessings, making no distinction in this life between believers and unbelievers; the obedient and the rebellious.

Ibn Arabi, explaining that the station of "friend" (*halil*) requires such behavior, concludes thus: "To behave in this way shows that one is favored by God. Therefore, whoever conducts themselves in such a way toward people, their "friendship" with God becomes true and authentic."[67] In fact, God Almighty commanded Abraham: "O my Halil (friend)! Behave ethically and justly toward everyone, including unbelievers."[68]

The Prophet Muhammad, peace be upon him, who made this Abrahamic social ethic an important cornerstone of Islam, said: "Avoid the imprecation of the aggrieved, even if he (or she) is an unbeliever. For there is no veil between God and the plea of the aggrieved. ... His (unbelief and) sin is his own concern (it cannot justify your oppression)."[69] Indeed it was this ethic of justice which, when implemented carefully, attracted non-Muslims to Islam in crowds, so that wherever Muslims went, there were masses of local people who also entered Islam. A priest who became upset with Muslims for attracting Christians with their morality and compassion said: "Fleeing from the tyranny of the Romans, 3,000 Christians have become Muslim. O mercy! You are worse than betrayal. For the Turks are buying the religion of the Christians by showing them kindness and compassion, not by forcing them to convert."[70]

RELENTLESSNESS IN STRUGGLING AGAINST HIS ENEMIES

While the Prophet Abraham is an example of the highest degree of lenience, mercy, and compassion, he did not fall into the mistake of making concessions when under enemy attack. We know this from his declaration to the people who opposed him and his followers:

> "We are quit of you and whatever you worship instead of God. We have absolutely rejected your polytheism, and there has arisen between us and you hostility and hate for ever until you believe in God alone (as the only One to be worshipped)." (Mumtahina 60:4)

This verse is one which requires a closer look. Just before this declaration by Abraham and those who followed him, we find this admonition spoken by God Almighty:

> Indeed, you have a good example in Abraham and those who follow him, when they said unto their (idolatrous) people...

Analyzing the story of his evident challenge against the people he lived among, in the light of this last sentence, we can reach the following conclusions:

1- This occurrence—Abraham's clear and even provocative reaction—must have taken place after he had been thrown into the fire but before he went into exile, because the verse refers to "those who were with" the Prophet Abraham. Based on what is known from narrations about the Prophet Abraham's life in various sources, it is believed that up until the attempted execution by fire, no one could be found who believed or followed him. It was after this miracle that some people like Sarah who had the great fortune of becoming his wife, and Prophet Lot, joined him and accepted faith in One God.

2- This Qur'anic verse also orders us to follow the Prophet Abraham's example in this. The question may arise, "When religion counsels and admonishes reasoning with people and 'debating in the best way,'[71] what is the place of such firmness as found in this passage?" My answer to this is, "These two approaches must be understood according to separate requirements for different circumstances." Establishing dialogue is an approach that is useful in an environment where intellectual struggle (debate) is possible, such as today's circumstances in the West. Yet it is possible that one's debate partner may not be convinced by good advice and a reasoned exchange. The political stance to be taken in such a situation is explained in the Surat al-Kafirun:

...Nor am I the one who is or will be the worshipper of that which you worship. And nor are you of those who are or will be worshippers of Him Whom I worship. You have your own din (with whatever it will bring you), and I have my own din (with whatever it will bring me). (Kafirun 109:4-6)[72]

Throughout history, in keeping with this principle, all Islamic states—even the most powerful—have avoided forcing non-Muslim citizens living in their territories to convert to Islam. There has never been a time or place where it can be said that a people was massacred because they refused to convert to Islam. The rule laid down in the Qur'an, "There shall be no coercion in matters of faith,"[73] was revealed specifically in reference to non-Muslims.[74] This means that God does not desire or allow us to bring people into Islam through coercion or threats. The application of this verse is one of the most honorable aspects of Islamic history.

Thus the behavior of the Prophet Abraham in the verse shows his ability to stand firm before a people whose maltreatment of him—in the name of their unbelief—knew no bounds, even to the point of trying to take his life. Before such ferocious opposition he made no concessions, and was not bent or broken by their persecution. In such conditions, if he had used a gentle manner and tried to reason with tyrannical oppressors this could have been interpreted as a surrender or at least weakness; it would mean yielding to defeat. In such a case, when under the attack of ruthless and tactless opponents, the Prophet Abraham exemplified the most appropriate response with the dignity and gravity required by the situation.

This is an Abrahamic message with great significance for our time.

EMIGRATION FOR THE SAKE OF GOD

It is essential to practice and implement God's orders. Thus, normal life cannot continue in a place which makes it impossible to practice religion. Emigration is commanded in the Qur'an from such a place to another area, and even says that those who do not emigrate in such circumstances lack strength in faith.[75] This was the reason the Companions of the Cave left their people to seek refuge in the cave.

For prophets, it is necessary not only to practice God's orders, but also to teach it to other people. For instance, as long as it was possible to communicate and teach his message, Prophet Muhammad continued his life in Mecca, bearing all kinds of difficulties and persecution. When the pressure and persecution of the idolaters of Mecca increased as they attempted to stop him from teaching the revelation, the Prophet's legal protector—his uncle Abu Talib—came to him and said: "O nephew! My people came to me and complained about you... don't get both of us into trouble, don't give me a burden too heavy to carry..." The Messenger of God, thinking that his uncle was considering retracting his protection, replied: "If you were even to put the sun in my right hand, and the moon in the left, I will never give up preaching my cause!"

In other words, the Messenger of God clearly rejected the safety of protection if this protection meant he could not convey the Message.[76] When his uncle and protector died, the circumstances changed for him in Mecca; it was no longer possible for him to teach about Islam. He began looking for other ways to convey his message, and with this motive went to Taif. He met with the leaders of Taif one by one, requesting their protection and support.

I would like to emphasize here that the Prophet was not asking them to save his life; rather, he was asking for their help to make it possible to fulfill his duty. Ibn Hisham tells the story thus: "Prophet Muhammad, peace be upon him, called them to God, and at the same time asked them to help Islam have a chance to spread by protecting it against aggressive opposition."[77] Since this attempt brought no positive results, he negotiated with the people of Medina for an opportunity to convey the message of Islam there, and decided to emigrate from Mecca.

In summary, it is important to recognize and keep in mind that, both for messengers of God and—when necessary—for believers, emigration is a serious and important life experience undertaken to fulfill one's duties to God.[78]

Likewise, the Prophet Abraham decided to emigrate in order to save his faith and his freedom to worship God Almighty,[79] and thus emigration for such purposes became an Abrahamic message to humanity. After the attempted execution by fire, he left his country, saying: "Now I am going to emigrate purely for my Lord's sake (in full conviction that) He will guide me (to a land where I will be able to worship Him freely)" (Saffat 37:99).

According to one of the narrations of Tabari, the place the Prophet Abraham left was Babylon.[80] The followers of the Prophet Abraham accompanied him in his emigration. After his miraculously surviving the fire, some people believed in his message, though it is not clear how many. His wife Sarah and his brother Haran's son Lot are assumed to be among those who believed in his message after the fire.[81] Even though Tabari says that many people believed in the Prophet Abraham, his words to his wife, "There is no one besides us in this world who believes," indicate that his followers were few (despite the belief of Prophet Lot) during their difficulties in Egypt that arose from the Pharaoh's attempts to harm him.[82]

The Prophet Abraham did not stay long in Egypt; he returned to Palestine. As I mentioned in earlier descriptions of his life, he arrived in Hebron and sent Lot, who later became the prophet of Sodom, to Jordan. Soon afterward, he moved to a place called Bethel between Ramla and Jerusalem. He began to amass some wealth and continued to strive to spread the message of Islam.

A COMMUNITY IN HIMSELF

One of the most interesting verses of the Qur'an regarding the virtues of the Prophet Abraham is the one that describes him as a community:

> Abraham was a community (umma) sincerely obedient to God
> as a man of pure faith (free from unbelief, associating partners

with God and hypocrisy), and he was not of the idolaters."
(Nahl 16:120)

Umma comes from the same root as *imam*, the leader of the community. Thus "the *Umma* of Muhammad" means "those who follow Prophet Muhammad." In this context it also means a society or nation. In some hadith, Prophet Muhammad used the term "*umma*" for certain individuals, such as Zayd ibn Amr ibn Nufayl[83] and Qus ibn Sa'id. For instance, he said of Qus, "He will be resurrected on the Day of Judgment alone as an *umma*." Ibn al-Athir interpreted *umma* here as a person who has a *din* (religion, faith, moral code), supporting this opinion with the above verse about the Prophet Abraham.[84]

However, the use of the word *umma* for the Prophet Abraham in this verse has been interpreted in various ways by different scholars. According to the fourth of Fahreddin Razi's four opinions, the *umma* of the Prophet Abraham reached a unique and honorable level of faith and religion. Since the Prophet Abraham's message was the reason his *umma* became important, he himself was called an "*umma*."[85]

As Razi also notes, the explanation that "he is called "*umma*" because he was a true believer when all other people were unbelievers" is weak, since, although he was alone at the beginning, so many people and so many nations later entered his religion. What makes him worthy of this title is the absolutely unique degree of his faith, patience, trust in God, and submission to the will of God.

Here it is also important to say that, keeping in mind the Prophet Abraham's compassion for his family and his mercifulness and tender-heartedness toward his followers, it is also possible that he was called an "*umma*" due to his struggle and compassion for his community.

It could be that the Almighty referred to him with the word "*umma*" because as the patron/guardian of his people he carried a great responsibility.

This sense of guardianship, putting others first, and giving importance to their happiness, security, and peace of mind is in a way similar to the virtues of tenderness and mercy. The following quote from Nursi shows what an exceptional degree the Prophet Abraham had of this sense: "Whoever is the protector and helper of a nation is a nation himself."[86] This means the Prophet Abraham displayed an exemplary level of concern for all believers, and even all people, always working for their guidance to the straight path and facing many difficulties and dangers. Thus his being called *umma* by God expresses the depth of Abraham's concern and care in this sense. In fact, showing truly boundless compassion, he did not lose his soft-heartedness toward his people and his desire for them to be guided to righteousness even after they had tried to execute him and had exiled him; some prophets such as Noah and Moses cursed their people in such situations. Instead, he kept asking for God's mercy and forgiveness for those who would not follow the path of righteousness, until it became absolutely certain that they would never do so. Since God Almighty's mercy is greater than His wrath,[87] perhaps His referring to the Prophet Abraham as an *"umma* in himself" shows God's pleasure at and recognition of the prophet's great mercy and compassion toward his people. Taken in context, this also suggests that, although the feelings and actions of Prophets Noah and Moses were also legitimate, the response of the Prophet Abraham, who was able to show more compassion than they, was more pleasing and preferable to God, and thus serves as the better example.

I would like to reiterate here how important a part this attribute constituted in his personality: the Old Testament also calls the Prophet Abraham a nation. Once more we find there: "The Lord said unto Abraham, 'I will make of you a great nation, and I will bless you...'" (Genesis 12:1-3).

This shows a clear path to those who want to follow in the path of the Prophet Abraham and to take him as an example: the way to attain a spirituality and morality as great as a nation is, throwing aside selfishness, to always work for one's people and nation, helping them to pass through difficulties and troubles, and undergoing sacrifices for them, thus to be elevated above one's individual self to the level of a nation and people.

CONCERN FOR HIS FAMILY AND DESCENDANTS

One of the foremost things associated with the Prophet Abraham is his family and descendants. There are several verses in the Qur'an about his closeness to his family.[88]

Secondly, God Almighty, in parallel with the intimate bond between him and his family, blessed Abraham's descendants in a unique way, raising them to a station of honor. For this reason, Muslims mention the mercy shown to the Prophet Abraham and his family when asking God for mercy for Prophet Muhammad and his family in each of the five daily prayers: "O, Our Sustainer! Have mercy on Prophet Muhammad and his family as you had mercy on the Prophet Abraham and his family."

It is a great honor and immeasurable distinction for the Prophet Abraham and his family to be remembered in every daily prayer of all Muslims, which is the most important pillar of Islam. Nursi explained why the Prophet Abraham is remembered with such a prayer, although the Prophet Muhammad was far ahead of him in mercy, pointing out that many prophets came from the line of the Prophet Abraham: "For sure Prophet Abraham was not equal to Prophet Muhammad (peace and blessings be upon them), but his family or descendants were prophets. Muhammad's, peace be upon him, family were saints, and saints cannot reach the level of the prophets."[89]

Such descendants, honored with the light of the prophets and prophethood, were a blessing in answer to his prayers. The importance of his prayers was due to the importance of his place before God, being *Halilullah,* the Friend of God. When the Prophet Abraham reached the station of this Friendship, as a result of his success in all his tests and trials, and reaching through them the purest form of faith in God (*tawhid*), he used his unique position as a chance to pray for his family and descendants. He asked for righteous people to come from his blood-line until the end of time to be the spiritual and material leaders of humanity and that they be followed and accepted by their people.

Here I would like to clarify something: The importance that the Prophet Abraham gave to his descendants was not nationalism or tribalism as they are understood today. It was a serious drive toward establishing the unity of humanity as he established faith in the unity of God. People of various races, languages, and cultures associate themselves with the Prophet Abraham and know him as their own. The importance of this for humanity should not be underestimated.

The fact that all those within the circle of Islam identify themselves as part of the "nation of Abraham" has contributed greatly to the unity of Muslims under one governmental authority until the beginning of the twentieth century.

I believe that in the future, a global peace that can embrace all of humanity will be achieved through the development of unity of the followers of the major world religions—particularly Jews, Christians and Muslims—with conscious agreement that they are members of the same Abrahamic community. For the Qur'an tells us that both Jews and Christians, no less than Muslims, are the inheritors of the Prophet Abraham and have the right to proudly follow him.

GOD-GIVEN VIRTUES

In expounding on the exemplary virtues of the Prophet Abraham, I would like to re-emphasize that these virtues were a consequence of his free-will choices and struggles. He always turned to God Almighty, to righteousness and truth and the Straight Path, with his free personal choice and continuous perseverance; on this path he developed and increased his patience and experience. Thus, God Almighty gave him certain extraordinary virtues and qualities as a reward for his choice to persevere and struggle and made his life an example for generations to come. As previously indicated, the same point is stated in the Qur'an as:

> ...his Lord tested Abraham with severe commandments... and he fulfilled them thoroughly.... (Baqara 2:124)

Later in the same verse, after the Prophet Abraham passed all the tests and trials given to him, God Almighty rewards him by saying, "I will make you a leader of humanity." Some scholars have concluded from this verse that prophethood came to the Prophet Abraham after all his challenges and trials, reasoning thus: "This verse shows that all the Prophet Abraham's challenges and tests were before his prophethood; God Almighty gave him leadership—or prophethood—after he had succeeded in all of them one by one."

Al-Qadi, who also takes this line, emphasizes that all tests and experiences which were meant to differentiate the capabilities of human beings were given to the Prophet Abraham before his Prophethood, since "going through all these phases seems to be the reason God Almighty assigned him as a leader/prophet. Obviously his success occasioned this appointment, so the tests and trials must have come before the Prophethood."[90] However, other scholars are of the opinion that he dealt with all these difficult tests after he became a Prophet, arguing that "he could only have succeeded through revealed knowledge, and this requires his receiving revelation before facing these responsibilities." Razi does not underestimate the opinion of al-Qadi, seeing it as valuable for comparison. Although he does not overtly disagree with him, it can be said that he accepts a middle way between the two opinions: that the Prophet Abraham's reasoning with the stars, moon, and sun occurred before he became a Prophet, while his other tests were afterward.[91]

BEING A CHOSEN ONE

The following Qur'anic verse calls the Prophet Abraham one of the few chosen people honored as such by all Creation, and asks the Prophet Muhammad to remember him with this attribute:

> And remember Our servants Abraham and Isaac and Jacob, endowed with power (in obedience to God and doing good deeds), and insight (to discern the truth in things and events). We made them perfectly pure and sincere by virtue of a characteristic most pure: their constant remembrance of the Abode

(of the Hereafter). They are in Our sight among the perfectly
purified, chosen ones, the truly good. (Sad 38:45-47)

The Prophet Abraham's "chosenness" (being among the elect)
is not only an honor for this world, but also for the Hereafter. There
he will be honored because he is "among the righteous":

...Indeed, We chose him as one pure and most distinguished in
the world, and he is surely among the righteous in the Hereafter.
(Baqara 2:130)

INSIGHT INTO GOD'S MIGHTY DOMINION

The Prophet Abraham was distinguished and honored by God before
all the worlds, which can be seen in several of the unique blessings
he received. One of these special favors of God is proclaimed in this
verse:

Thus did We show Abraham (the ugliness and irrationality of
polytheism and) the inner dimension of existence and eternal
truth which this outer, corporeal dimension manifests and depends
upon—this We did to the end that he might attain the final certainty of belief (according to his capacity). (An'am 6:75)

Abraham was shown *malakut*. It is translated here as the "inner
dimension of existence and eternal truth." We can also define *malakut*
as "the inner dimension, where Divine Power operates directly"[92]
and "the inner or transparent aspect of things, that shows their
Maker." Here is one of Nursi's explanations about *malakut*:

"Divine Power operates in the inner, spiritual dimension of things
(the metaphysical kingdom). Like a mirror, the universe has two sides:
corporeal (resembling a mirror's colored face) and metaphysical
(resembling the mirror's shining face and looking to the Creator).
Opposites exist in the corporeal side, which manifests beauty and ugliness, good and bad, big and small, difficulty and ease. The Majestic
Creator of the universe veils His Power's acts behind the veil of
observed causes so that those who lack understanding do not regard
His Power's relation to simple things as unbecoming to Him. His

Honor and Majesty require this. Causes have no real effect upon creation, for that would violate His Oneness and Unity. The metaphysical world, absolutely clear and transparent, contains none of the physical world's grossness. As Divine Power operates directly there, cause and effect have no effect, obstacles cannot interfere, and creating a particle is as easy as forming a sun."[93]

In other words, it is the aspect of natural law which brings together atoms, giving them shape, giving things a character and a purpose. This aspect is taken for granted and veiled by familiarity; consciously observing it gives true and unshakeable knowledge of the Creator of all things. This blessing of being shown the "*malakut* of heavens and earth" could be the reason the Prophet Abraham was able to develop such a perfect *tawhid* and rise to an elevated level of faith.

This elevated spiritual station was not given to every prophet, which makes it all the more extraordinary. Thus, this gift of seeing the *malakut* was a special honor for the Prophet Abraham, like the *miraj* (the miraculous Ascension) of the Prophet Muhammad.[94] On this *miraj*, Prophet Muhammad was led through the layers of the Heavens and saw that each of the major eight prophets had been placed at different "levels"; if this showed the spiritual level they were each able to attain, then the Prophet Abraham was the very highest, given that he was seen in the seventh level.[95] Ibn Abu Jamra wrote, "The position of the *Halil* or "friend" of God must be the highest level of spiritual attainment. The only higher would be the *habib* or "beloved" of God, which describes Prophet Muhammad. Accordingly during his *miraj*, the latter passed the point which no other, including the Prophet Abraham, was able to pass, into the direct presence of God."[96]

FRIENDSHIP TO GOD ALMIGHTY

One of the virtues of the Prophet Abraham mentioned in the Qur'an is that he gained God's "friendship." He is called "Halilullah," which means an "intimate friend of God." In order to understand this term better, we must consult the dictionary meaning of *halil*. According to one explanation, the word comes from the root "*hilal*," which literally means "distance," or the gap between two things. Extrapolating from this, one's "*halil*" is a person who is an "insider" in one's business, a confidante; it also means the *halil* is one who is wholeheartedly beloved.

According to Ibn Hajar's explanation, "*halil*" comes from the root "*hullat*," which means loyalty; thus the love that enters a heart is also called "*hullat*." This meaning makes more sense when considering the love of God in the Prophet Abraham's heart. The reverse can also be understood (Abraham was the beloved of God). In sum, "*Halilullah*" means a person whom God Almighty greatly loves.[97] Since every sincere believer's ultimate goal is to gain the love and pleasure of God, this term not only expresses the degree to which he was elevated, but also conveys the importance of investigating how he came to gain such an esteemed honor, his perseverance in this journey, the virtues he possessed which allowed him to reach such a point, the spiritual values for which he stood, the messages he brought, etc. At the same time, this is very significant for people who follow the messages of the Prophet Abraham: they have the opportunity to gain the pleasure of God with more certainty and less difficulty.

The verse that calls the Prophet Abraham the "friend of God" is in the fourth *sura* of the Qur'an: "God exalted Abraham with His love (made him *halil*)" (Nisa 4:125). The Prophet Abraham gained this position by establishing the *hanif* religion (the faith in one God, as explained earlier) among people and implementing it to the highest degree in his personal life as well as in the circle of his family.[98] The Qur'an gives the message that "whoever implements this straight (*hanif*) path as he did, will reach the highest stations attainable in religion."[99]

THE PEACE AND BLESSINGS OF GOD UPON THE PROPHET ABRAHAM

The achievement of the Prophet Abraham, which brought him to be honored as "chosen" and "a friend of God," also gained him the specific greeting and blessing of God. In the Qur'an God says: "Peace be upon Abraham!" (Saffat 37:109) This kind of greeting is also addressed to Prophet Noah, Prophet Moses, Prophet Aaron, and Prophet Elias (peace be upon all of them). This achievement represents the direction of God and a high compliment to the recipient, and it is significant that the Prophet Abraham is among those who are honored with this exceptional blessing.

Thus people who strive to follow the example of the Prophet Abraham have the chance to receive a similar blessing from God.

HAVING A CHILD IN OLD AGE

A detail of one of the longer histories of the Prophet Abraham related in the Qur'an gives the hope and the message that it is possible to have a child, even at a very advanced age, something that is traditionally considered to be impossible.

According to this detail, the Prophet Abraham was visited by the angels that were on their way to punish the people of Lot. During their visit, they gave the good news of conception of Prophet Isaac to the Prophet Abraham's wife Sarah. She was surprised by their seemingly impossible news, and described her feelings thus:

> She said: "Oh, woe is me! Shall I bear a child, now that I am an old woman, and this my husband is an old man? That would be a strange thing indeed! They (the envoys) said: "Are you surprised at God's command? The mercy of God and His blessings be upon you, O people of the house!" (Hud 11:72-74)

THE SCROLLS OF ABRAHAM

One of the God-given virtues of the Prophet Abraham is that he was given Scrolls (Revelation) by God. The Qur'an mentions these Scrolls in two different places.[100] Some details regarding the Scrolls are found in these verses and some hadith. Here, I would like to call attention to the fact that the Scrolls signify an important way God favored Abraham.

DISTINGUISHED DESCENDANTS

A fact that increases the importance of the Prophet Abraham is his honorable line of descendants, which will continue until the end of time. As I mentioned before, his descendants were made to be distinguished before all of Creation throughout history. Scholars agree that the unique superiority of his lineage is that from it came a line of Prophets. The privilege of having a unique line of descendants was the result of his praying for this after he had succeeded in obeying some commands God gave him to test him. God Almighty accepted this prayer from him:

> ... his Lord tested Abraham with severe commandments and terrible ordeals, and that he fulfilled them thoroughly. (Then his Lord) declared: "Indeed I will make you an Imam for all people." He appealed: "My offspring also?" (His Lord) answered: "(I will appoint among those who deserve. But) My covenant does not include the wrongdoers."(Baqara 2:124)

In other verses it is more explicitly expressed that the Prophet Abraham was given a unique line of descendants as a result of his prayer, and among them would also be "evildoers":

> God made pure Adam and Noah and the House of Abraham and the House of Imran, choosing them above all humankind."(Al Imran 3:33-34)

> We did grant the Family of Abraham (including the progeny of Ishmael who descended from him, as well as that of Isaac) the Book and the Wisdom, and We granted them a mighty kingdom (in both the material and spiritual realm). (Nisa 4:54)

In this verse too it is mentioned that from the distinguished line of descendants would also come evil people:

> Indeed We sent Noah and Abraham as Messengers, and established in their line Prophethood and the Book. Among them (their offspring) there have been those who have followed the right guidance, but many among them have been transgressors. (Hadid 57:26)

Prophet Muhammad, too, said that some mischief-makers would come out of his bloodline, who would call themselves his family through their blood relation to him. In reality, he said, such people would have no kinship with him, but instead those who are God-conscious would be his family.[101] This important concept is also confirmed with a verse in the Qur'an related to the son of Prophet Noah:

> "O Noah! He (being an unbeliever) is not of your family. He is one of unrighteous conduct (which embodied his unbelief)." (Hud 11:46)

Sayyid Qutb, taking the concept a little too literally, interprets the verse: "In reality, kinship is not based on blood relationship, but only on faith and religion."[102]

In my opinion, instead of completely denying the ties of blood kinship, it would be more appropriate to take away from this verse an emphasis on the importance of relation based on faith.

THE RELATION BETWEEN ABRAHAM AND PROPHET MUHAMMAD

I mentioned previously that when the Prophet Abraham prayed that leaders of men should come from his descendants, God Almighty accepted it, yet stated that there would also be some evildoers from his line. It is because of his sincere prayer and God's blessing upon that prayer that the Prophet Abraham received the title "the Father of Prophets" and became the ancestor of the Prophet Muhammad. Moreover, almost all of the Prophets whose names are mentioned in the Qur'an after the Prophet Abraham are his descendants. Prophet Muhammad has a unique place among those prophets. This connection honors the Prophet Abraham, and vice versa: the Prophet Muhammad was proud of belonging to his family.

When Prophet Muhammad was once addressed as "the most auspicious person to emerge from humankind," he countered, "that is the Prophet Abraham," attributing that virtue to him.[103] Often when he mentioned an aspect of his personality, he would link it to the Prophet Abraham—for example, one of his sayings: "My Sustainer made me a "friend" to Himself, as He made the Prophet Abraham."[104]

When the Prophet Abraham was thrown into the fire, he said, "God is enough for me; and how excellent a guardian He is!" and the fire did not harm him. Prophet Muhammad gave the same response after the Battle of Uhud, when Mecca started circulating propaganda against the Muslims to discourage and weaken them, saying: "Behold, a host has gathered against you, therefore be alarmed by them."[105] With his answer (the words of the Prophet Abraham) their faith was strengthened. With newfound courage they even said to the Meccans at the end of the battle, "meet us again next year to fight," but when they went to the designated place the next year the Meccans did not come. It was these words that inspired and motivated the Muslim army while the Meccans felt impending defeat.[106] The Prophet Abraham introduced to humanity the only religion acceptable in the sight of God, complete submission to the will of God (*islam*) in its basic form; he also exemplified its perfect achievement. Prophet Muhammad gave Islam its final form by responding to the needs of humanity in many areas of life which had become more advanced and sophisticated, and accordingly adding practical judgment and applications.

FATHER OF FIRSTS

Another virtue of the Prophet Abraham is having been the "father" of many initiatives in history.

- The tradition of circumcision was introduced by the Prophet Abraham.
- He was the first person to host guests.[107]
- He was the first person to cook meat stew.[108]
- He was the first person to see his hair turn white: Even though people before him obviously also had white hair, the reason why the Prophet Abraham was symbolically "first" is that the story of his hair turning white became an important and timeless message: "Abraham asked for an auspi-

cious sign from his Sustainer. As a result, two-thirds of his hair turned white. Shocked, he asked, "What is this?" He was told, "This is a sign in this world, and a light in the Hereafter."[109]

What could be more beneficial to any person than remembering old age and death? For this reason, Prophet Muhammad told his companions it was better not to take out their white hairs, for they would be a light to their owner in the Hereafter.[110]

- Because he was the first person to wear the loose-fitting trousers,[111] he will be the first person clothed on the Day of Judgment, while everyone else will be barefoot and naked.[112] Another source also says he will be clothed first as a way of honoring his virtue before all people.[113]

- It is a narrated in a tradition that the first Arabic speaking person was Prophet Ishmael when he was at the age of thirteen.[114] This is also significant in better understanding the importance of Prophet Abraham who was Ishmael's father.

- He initiated many acts of bodily cleanliness, such as washing the mouth and nose, brushing the teeth, trimming the mustache, shaving excess hair and pubic hair, cutting nails, washing between the fingers, circumcision, washing the private parts after using the bathroom, as well as others.[115]

- Individual liability in law was first introduced by Prophet Abraham.

PART THREE

The Service of the Prophet Abraham

The phrase, "the service of Prophet Abraham," is used to refer to all the beneficial things that this prophet did for humanity, both at the intellectual level and at the application level. In this section, this service will be discussed under various sub-titles. For instance, his legacy of achievements includes not only the construction of the Ka'ba (the house of worship), but also the institution of the entire hajj, including its rituals; even the methodology that he followed in teaching them is still used today. All of these I perceive as services, both as models and messages for us. Yet, in order to better explain the types of service I have enumerated here, as well as some I have not yet mentioned, and to emphasize the importance of certain issues, I have divided them into different subsections.

SERVICE RELATED TO THE HAJJ

One of the five Pillars of Islam, the Hajj, has a unique connection with Prophet Abraham. He has been linked to everything from the construction of the Ka'ba, which is circumambulated during pilgrimage, to determining the elements of pilgrimage and instituting the practice of slaughtering an animal afterward.

THE CONSTRUCTION OF THE KA'BA

There are some traditions which state that the history of the Ka'ba stretches back to Prophet Adam.[1] According to these narrations, during the time of Prophet Abraham, the location of the Ka'ba was on a little hill, both sides of which were eroded by floods.[2] But the important thing for us is that it was later constructed by Prophet Abraham.

God Almighty commanded Prophet Abraham to build the Ka'ba,[3] as a purified place of worship. Abraham did so with his son Ishmael who traveled from Damascus to Mecca to help with the construction.[4] After the Ka'ba had been built, God commanded Prophet Abraham and Ishmael to maintain it, and in particular, to "Purify My House for those who go around It as an act of devotion, and those who abide in devotion, and those who bow and prostrate themselves (in Prayer)."[5]

When Prophet Abraham received this directive, he prayed:

> My Lord! Make this land (Mecca) secure, and preserve me and my children (my sons and their descendants) from ever worshipping idols. (Ibrahim 14:35)

God accepted his prayer[6] and ordered that Prophet Abraham start practicing pilgrimage on earth:

> Publicly proclaim the (duty of) Pilgrimage for all humankind, that they come to you on foot and on lean camels, coming from every far-away point, So that they may witness all benefits in store for them, and offer during the known, appointed days the sacrificial cattle that He has provided for them by pronouncing God's Name over them. Eat of their meat and feed the distressed, the poor. Thereafter let them tidy themselves up, and fulfill the vows, and go round the Most Ancient, Honorable House in devotion. (Hajj 22:27-29)

According to hadith, after receiving this order from God, Prophet Abraham and Prophet Ishmael visited various tribes and invited them to the pilgrimage, saying: "O mankind! A house of worship (Bayt) has been built for you; come to visit it!" God made this invitation so effective that whoever received it—not only human beings, but everything, including stones, trees, and animals—all said: "*Labbayk! Allahumma labbayk! (O God! Here I am at your service!)*"[7]

Here it is relevant to note that the practice of pilgrimage also exists in the other two Abrahamic religions, Judaism and Christianity.

According to Tabarani, the Jewish and Christian pilgrimages took place on the same dates as the hajj Prophet Muhammad undertook with his followers.[8]

The angel Gabriel taught Prophet Abraham the rituals that comprise the pilgrimage.[9]

As we will see, the following verse of the Qur'an shows that all aspects of the Pilgrimage, from the construction of the Ka'ba to the choice of its rituals and other locations which are also visited during the hajj, are related to Prophet Abraham, as they were either initiated by him or commemorate him. The introduction of the verse, as it declares the honor and preeminence of the Ka'ba built by Abraham, has a unique meaning and importance for our discussion here:

> Behold, the first House (of Prayer) established for humankind is the one at Becca (Mecca), a blessed place and a (center or focus of) guidance for all peoples. In it there are clear signs (demonstrating that it is a blessed sanctuary, chosen by God as the center of guidance), and the Station of Abraham. Whoever enters it is in security (against attack and fear). Pilgrimage to the House is a duty owed to God by all who can afford a way to it. And whoever refuses (the obligation of the Pilgrimage) or is ungrateful to God (by not fulfilling this command), God is absolutely independent of all creatures. (Al Imran 3:96-97)

According to some traditions, during the construction of the Ka'ba, when the height of the wall reached a certain point, it became very difficult to lift the stones and place them on the walls. Thus, Prophet Abraham was given a stepping stone, which is probably what this verse refers to "The Station of Abraham." It is also mentioned in some hadiths. The footprint of the Prophet Abraham is preserved on that stone.[10]

Prophet Abraham's prayer was indeed accepted: from his time to the present the Ka'ba has continued to be a place for the faithful to visit and worship. And those who go to circumambulate the Ka'ba do so in complete security, remembering with love and respect the one who built it.

STONING SATAN

The ritual of "stoning Satan," which is part of the hajj pilgrimage, is a commemoration and re-enactment of an episode involving Prophet Abraham. According to a tradition from Ibn Abbas, when Prophet Abraham was commanded to perform the pilgrimage, Angel Gabriel took him to the valley of Aqaba. There, Satan appeared and tried to stop him. Prophet Abraham threw seven stones at Satan, who then disappeared. When Prophet Abraham arrived in the valley, Satan appeared before him again. He threw seven more stones and Satan left him alone.[11]

Imam Ghazali, in his work *Ihya*, summarizes the lesson that is contained in performing this ritual: "To perform worship because God commanded it, not because its meaning and deeper significance is understood intellectually." He also writes: "Throwing the stones, without reasoning or using judgment, should be done simply because it is the command of God, with consciousness of one's servanthood and thus the intention of obeying God's command. The intention to resemble Prophet Abraham, "Friend of God," is also important. For in this place Satan appeared to Prophet Abraham in order to cause him to rebel, or to otherwise fail, in pilgrimage. With the command of God, he stoned Satan. If you say, "Prophet Abraham saw Satan and stoned him, yet he has not appeared to me, so my action is accomplishing nothing," be aware that this thought is also from Satan. Be sure that, even though you seemingly throw those stones at pre-determined spots, in reality, with those stones you break Satan's back and get him out of your heart. For what really breaks Satan's back is to do your duty out of respect and obedience to the Most High God, because it is God's command—even when you don't understand the wisdom of this act."[12]

Running between the hills of Safa and Marwa

Running between the hills of Safa and Marwa, which is another ritual of pilgrimage, commemorates events related to Hagar, the wife of Prophet Abraham. After Prophet Abraham had left Hagar and their baby son Ishmael near the Ka'ba, which was a deserted area at that time, Hagar left Ishmael and hurriedly climbed to the top of the hill of Safa to look for water while also keeping a watchful eye on her son. Yet she could not find any water. From there she ran to the hill of Marwa. She repeatedly dashed between the hills seven times for the sake of Ishmael, who was suffering from dehydration.

Her search was still unsuccessful. Deeply saddened, her heart filled with compassionate love for her son, Hagar said, "O Ishmael! At least don't let me watch you die; die while I look away!"

However, she realized that Ishmael was digging at the sand with his feet. She witnessed a miracle: A well sprang up from the spot where he was kicking. It was the well of Zamzam. She rushed to it and tried to cup it in her hands to keep it from spreading out and being lost. Prophet Muhammad, praising Hagar's action, said: "If she had not (prevented it from flowing freely), Zamzam would not have stayed a well, but would have become a creek instead."[13]

The Message of Hagar

There is an important message for believers in this pilgrimage ritual, which deserves some attention here. Mother Hagar continued running to find water for her son, repeating the dash between the two hills seven times without losing hope, even though initially she could not find anything. After the first few tries, she could have given up her search in despair, thinking, "this is the middle of a desert, there is no water here, we will perish." Instead, holding tenaciously to hope, she ran the same distance, perhaps retracing the very same steps, seven times. After the seventh, her deep sincerity was blessed with a manifestation of God's mercy. In the same way, when trying to bring about a righteous goal, believers should continue their struggle without falling into hopelessness, even if troubles come seven times over.

The second lesson to be drawn from the same instance is the necessity that all such difficult but worthy causes must be undertaken and continued in hope and determination, not in hopelessness and despair. To remind them of this principle, Prophet Muhammad instructed his companions to walk quickly during their first Pilgrimage, so that the Meccans who were watching the Muslims could not say of them, "These people are so exhausted, they can't do anything properly."

Sacrifice

Another ritual related to the hajj pilgrimage is the slaughter or "sacrifice" of an animal. This also commemorates an event in the life of Prophet Abraham. After remaining childless for a long time, he asked God Almighty to grant him the gift of a child who would be one of the righteous.[14] When the child became old enough to walk with his father, Prophet Abraham was shown in his dreams three times that he should sacrifice his son.[15]

After completing all the necessary preparations—some of which will be explained later under the title of "Abraham's Family"—Abraham laid his son Ishmael down on his side in order to sacrifice him to God. But to his surprise, the knife would not cut the boy's throat. Prophet Abraham tried again, yet the knife could not fulfill its function, having no permission from God to do so.

Prophet Abraham thus passed one of the most serious tests of his life: that of sacrificing his own child. Prophet Abraham, who had truly submitted himself to God, proved ready to give up not just one, but thousands of sons if he had had them. In fact, God Almighty had tested him in order to set him apart and exalt him. Immediately a ram was sent for Prophet Abraham to sacrifice in place of Ishmael.[16]

The Place of Sacrifice

The place of sacrifice, called Manhar, one of the sites associated with the Pilgrimage, is also associated with Prophet Abraham: it is said that it was here that Prophet Abraham laid Ishmael down to sacrifice him. Nevertheless it is also possible that the place of sacrifice was actually by the rock of Mina, or close to the masjid; it is also reported that it could have actually been the place where pilgrims sacrifice their animals today. [17]

The Days of Tashrik

The 11th, 12th and 13th days of the 12th lunar month, Dhu al-Hijjah, are called the "Days of Tashrik." These are also the 2nd, 3rd, and the 4th days of Eid al-Adha for Muslims. According to Islamic tradition these are the days of tribulation that Prophet Abraham suffered when he was asked to sacrifice his son. The anguish which he underwent because of his intention to fulfill God's every command was transformed by God into assurance. Ibn Abu Jamra expounds on this: "God transformed his tribulation into complete assurance. In this way those days became the most noble of days. When one of God's servants has been granted a blessing, it is never diminished, but rather increased. Moreover, it is made eternal."

The Days of Tashrik renew the legacy of the Prophet Abraham in commemorating him; and as he taught us, Muslims knock at the door of the Most Merciful with respect before our Lord's commands, saying in our prayers: "How great is our God Who has created all things beneficial and good for humanity and for us, even that which does not please our ego or that the meaning of which is hidden from our understanding; and only He is worthy of praise."

Ishmael or Isaac?

A different detail, while not of the greatest importance, is encountered in sources which deal with the topic at hand: which son was Prophet Abraham to sacrifice—Ishmael or Isaac?

Ali Ünal explains this in his study, *The Qur'an with Annotated Interpretation in Modern English*:

"The verse of the Bible (Genesis 22:2) which states that God ordered Abraham to sacrifice Isaac contradicts several other verses.

This verse mentions that when this order was given to Abraham, Isaac was his only son. Whereas, according to Genesis, 21:5, when Isaac was born, Abraham was 100 years old, and according to Genesis 16:16, Ishmael was born when Abraham was 86 years old. So according to the Bible, when Isaac came into the world, Ishmael was a young man of 14 years. This clearly shows that when Abraham was ordered to sacrifice his "only son" he was being ordered to sacrifice Ishmael."

Related to this issue, some scholars say that the son to be sacrificed could not have been Isaac, taking as proof a *hadith* of Prophet Muhammad which says "I am the descendent of two Sacrifices."[18]

REFLECTIONS ON SOME OF ABRAHAM'S MESSAGES

As previously explained, Prophet Abraham performed a great service to humanity with the many messages he brought, which are found not only in his virtues—both those he was blessed with and those he labored to develop—but also in the lessons implicit in the very service he performed. In this section, those messages which do not fall into any category previously mentioned or that will be handled later will be discussed.

Abandoning Imitation of Ancestors

According to the Qur'an, one of the most burdensome obstacles faced by nearly all the Prophets was the inclination of their people to imitate their ancestors. All their various peoples, when called by the Prophets to righteousness, used their desire to continue doing what their ancestors did as an unfailing pretext for defiance. Whether it was worshiping idols or committing any number of unseemly deeds, it seemed to them a credible excuse that their fathers had done the same.[19]

Prophet Abraham, during his prophetic mission, not only taught that it was wrong to worship idols, but also taught that the imitation of ancestors must be abandoned:

He said to his father and people: "What are these images to which you pay such sincere devotion?"
They said: "We have found our forefathers worshipping them."
"So, it is certain that," said he, "both of you, you and your forefathers, have been in obvious error." (Anbiya 21:52-54)[20]

From the beginning of his prophethood until the end of his life, the Prophet Abraham repeated over and over again that unthinkingly imitating ancestors is erroneous, comparing it to the "blind leading the blind." This was one of the central points of Abraham's teaching. Instead of the erroneous, dark ways of your ancestors, emulate your true forefather (Prophet Abraham), and follow the way of peace and submission that he taught. Strive in God's cause and purely for His sake (against His enemies to raise His Word, and against Satan and your carnal, evil-commanding souls,) in a manner worthy of that striving. He has chosen you (especially for this task) and has not laid any hardship on you in the Religion. This is the way of your father Abraham.

Islam—to keep humanity from falling into a loop of imitation as past peoples have done—set at peoples' head Prophets who exemplified the highest human virtues, and commanded that their path be followed. Islam made it clear that wherever possible, it is best to make *ijtihad*[21] or reason things through (based on trustworthy sources of information, such as the Prophets) rather than to unthinkingly mimic others in a vicious cycle.

Prophet Abraham was one of the first trailblazers on this path, an important leader in the fight against blind imitation.

Splendor in the World

Prophet Abraham was rewarded for his success in the various tests he underwent, not only with spiritual blessings, but with a number of physical, worldly blessings as well. In expounding on this topic, Razi explains that all the difficulties Prophet Abraham had to face in this world were in time replaced with their opposite, then lists examples: "His people wanted to burn him to death because he was alone, having no family or followers; God obliterated his loneliness such that the world is now full of his descendants. When all those close to him, including his father Azar, proved contrary to his message and preferred their own crooked paths, God surrounded him with those who followed his path and called others to righteousness, and raised up from his line generations of believers, and prophets worthy to receive the very revelation of God's word. While he began with nothing to his name, no worldly goods nor station, God bestowed on him both; he came to possess so many herds that no one could count them. It was even said that just to protect these herds, he had twelve thousand dogs with golden collars. As regards his station, he was given such a respected position that whenever Muslims bless and pray for any of the other prophets, they also bless and pray for Abraham, and this has been ordained for all time to continue until the Last Day. In fact the Qur'an shows he was not well known at the beginning of his mission: "One named Abraham is speaking against our idols," said his people, and their words show that until this time he was as yet unknown.[22]

Trials of faith may not be logical

One of the most crucial messages in the incidents and episodes of Prophet Abraham's life as told in the Qur'an and *hadith* is that it is unwise to rely excessively on logic in trials and tests of faith. God Almighty may try a person with the most difficult of tribulations, but He never "burdens any soul except within its capacity."[23] Besides, there is always wisdom behind every such test. Prophet Abraham's tests are the best example of this. What conceivable logic can be found in his being commanded to leave his baby son Ishmael and wife Hagar without water in a forsaken desert, to sacrifice his son when he reached 13 years of age, to stone Satan, and so on? Saul's (Talut) soldiers serve as a similar example: when they were on the way to war with Goliath their test was that they were told not to drink water from a stream they passed. Those who drank failed the test.[24]

Prophet Abraham never asked *why*. He always showed his constancy, fortitude, and obedience by complying perfectly with these commands; he passed the tests and was raised to the position of *Halilullah*, the Friend of God.

Destiny cannot be interfered with

The story of Prophet Abraham's birth clearly illustrates the fact that a human being can not change their destiny by trying to take precautions. Nimrod received a warning from one of his magicians; the magician had had a dream in which a person in Nimrod's kingdom ended his rule and dominion, putting an end to injustice and unbelief.

To prevent this dramatic end, Nimrod convened a council, and made a decision on the advice of his counselors: all the male children born in the prophesied year would be killed, and new pregnancies would be prevented by seizing husbands and holding them far from their families. Here it is important to note that a similar dream about Prophet Moses prompted Pharaoh to take similar measures. That Pharaoh and Nimrod followed the same methods to contend against believers is deeply meaningful.

When the year prophesied by the magicians came, Nimrod summoned all the pregnant women in his kingdom and held them under surveillance. Azar's wife, Prophet Abraham's mother, was exempted from this, because no one in the town knew about her pregnancy. It was said that she was still such a young woman and her stomach did not protrude so much. In the month and year that had been named by the magicians, all children born were slaughtered. Abraham's mother, when the time for delivery approached, went secretly at night to one of the nearby caves. There, she brought Abraham into the world...."[25]

In an interesting coincidence, the Pharaoh also resorted to such measures, with similar results, and his efforts to prevent the foreseen coming of one who would interrupt his reign of injustice and disbelief were in vain. Slaughtering innocents, keeping mothers and fathers under surveillance, separating families; none of these can change the fate of oppressors. Oppression does not benefit the oppressors; on the contrary, the cries and curses of the oppressed ensure their destruction. Their only reward will be to remain under this curse until the Day of Judgment. Those they tried to oppose, like Abraham, Moses, Noah and Lot, continue to be—and will always be—remembered well.

With the example of Prophet Abraham, the Qur'an demonstrates the message of God Almighty to the faithful, which was revealed to humanity at the very beginning and will remain true until the end of time:

> And the unbelievers schemed; but God brought their scheming
> to naught; for God is above all schemers. (Al Imran 3:54)

True power is with God

The Qur'an relates another message of God Almighty, the All-Wise. He created this world in order to test us. There will be oppressors, unbelievers, tyrants, and dictators, and sometimes, as part of the test, we will find them holding power: never be intimidated before their power, wealth, means of prosecution, and imprisonment, before their multitude of weapons, their assassins, or whatever else they may utilize. Don't let their boasts and menacing cause you to despair. True power is with God. Cling to the source of righteousness, and strive to find and establish justice. Victory will belong, in the end, to the righteous.

Especially when the stories of prophets are considered in light of other analogies and symbols in the Qur'an, we can conclude with absolute certainty that God Almighty promises to give glory to the just, righteous, and God-conscious and to establish an eternal law that the righteous will be exalted in the end: *Do not, then, be faint of heart, nor grieve, for you are always the superior side if you are (true) believers* (Al Imran 3:139). This law cannot and will not be changed.

What is required of sincere believers, then, is not to fear or despair, but to believe and live according to this, and be patient and persevere. Furthermore it is for believers to be as strong as Prophet Abraham and not to deviate from his example in faith: not to deviate from pure intentions, sincerity, and true servanthood, even in the face of threats like being thrown into the fire. This is what his faith required. In terms of the Hereafter, even if death should result from these difficulties, it is still a benefit and accomplishment.

Indeed, if unbelieving oppressors should end the earthly life of a believer, that is not the end of that person's existence. The righteous who die on the path of God are martyrs, and martyrs do not die. On the contrary, even when one gives their life in the cause of truth, their life's work lives on, and the person lives on through those who continue to benefit from that work. Efforts in the cause of righteousness will endure until Doomsday itself. Hence, those who are alone, powerless, helpless, but righteous (people like Noah, Abraham, Moses), will always become victorious in the end. Oppressors, be they Pharaoh, Nimrod, or others who contend against the righteous, will be overcome. The Overwhelming One of Absolute Might has clearly ordained that the former will be exalted and the latter debased. Again, this is revealed in the Qur'an: *The (final, happy) outcome is in favor of the God-revering, pious* (Araf 7:128; Ta Ha 20:132; Hud 11:49; Qasas 28:83)

Feeling of security in reaching out to people

One of the most basic needs and drives of human life is the search for a feeling of security. This includes safety and surety for tomorrow, as well as guarantee of intangible things such as freedom of thought and belief, and protection of honor and dignity. The verse quoted above goes on to relate that Prophet Abraham reminded his followers of these important human needs:

> ...(Tell me,) then, which of the two parties has right to feel secure, if you have anything of knowledge?

> Those who have believed and not obscured their faith with any wrongdoing (of which, associating partners with God is the most

grave, unforgivable kind)—they are the ones for whom there is true security, and they are rightly guided. (Anam 6:81-82)

This passage, even as it teaches about the risks to security brought by unbelief, also reminds believers that simply having faith does not automatically bring perfection of action. It is a reminder that for true salvation faith alone is not enough; it must be accompanied by good deeds. Even good deeds are not sufficient if they are not consistent, as when they are sullied by atrocities or injustices.

This being the case, we can see another Abrahamic message in the prescription that is given constantly by the Qur'an for "faith and right action."

Kindliness in communicating the message

One of the Abrahamic messages in the Qur'an is a gentle manner in communicating the message to others. When calling people to the straight path or teaching them, Abraham always used a gentle style, and carefully avoided cruel, harsh, or hurtful words. Whenever he tried to convince his father to turn from idols he began with "Dear father!" taking the utmost care not to put himself over his father or make him feel patronized. He paid attention to this aspect of his speech when addressing the unbelieving people around him, and even Nimrod himself. In a *hadith* related by Abu Hurayra, Prophet Abraham was an agent and example sent to teach humanity the highest ethics and methods in communicating and winning hearts:

Almighty God instructed the Prophet of Prophets, Abraham, thus: "You are My *Halil* (friend): So be of good character, even when interacting with unbelievers! In this way you can enter the council of the righteous. For My decree will be fulfilled, "Those who have excellent character and ethics, I will bring close to My mercy." Munawi adds, "The Prophet Abraham followed this command of his Lord; indeed, none after him, except the Prophet Muhammad who came from his own esteemed lineage, was ever able to reach or excel the heights of good character and morality he reached."[26]

In fact, to approach others in a good-mannered way instead of a rough or ill-tempered fashion is a priority of importance everywhere in society and not a principle peculiar only to preachers and teachers; but it cannot be emphasized enough that it is vital in certain service capacities, such as instruction and educative communication, since—as Razi wrote—"harsh and hurtful words cause the addressee to object and take his leave, which does not harm the teacher, but the one he is trying to teach."[27]

Let us not forget that teaching to others is not the duty of teachers at schools only; all people are instructors and trainers in one way or another for everyone is either a mother or father.

Several Prophets mentioned in the Qur'an illustrate the importance of a gentle and careful communication style. In order to emphasize the importance of this Abrahamic message, I will cite two examples from the lives of Prophet Moses and Prophet Muhammad, peace be upon them:

God Almighty warns Moses and Aaron to use gentle speech when sending them to address the Pharaoh:

> Go, both of you, to the Pharaoh for he has exceedingly rebelled. But speak to him with gentle words, so that he might reflect and be mindful or feel some awe (of Me, and behave with humility).(Ta Ha 20:43-44)

It is noteworthy that in this verse it is ordered that "gentle words" be used when these prophets invite the Pharaoh to divine guidance, despite the latter being well-known for his fierce, cruel nature. Most importantly, God gave this order knowing fully that Pharaoh would not accept the invitation. Gentility was required even in approaching such a man, one of the most rebellious unbelievers in history. This bespeaks the fundamental principle of consideration and mildness in communication. If this principle was important in communicating with the Pharaoh, who went astray to the ultimate level, then we can infer that we should communicate God's message to the people in our day in gentle words, no matter their situation.

The second example is related to Prophet Muhammad, peace be upon him. In the verse mentioned earlier in another context, it is also indicated that the Prophet of Islam was blessed by God with an extraordinary ability to follow this Abrahamic principle, being considerate and gentle with everyone he spoke to.

> It was by a mercy from God that (at the time of the setback), you (O Messenger) were lenient with them (your Companions). Had you been harsh and hard-hearted, they would surely have scattered away from about you. Then pardon them, pray for their forgiveness, and take counsel with them in the affairs (of public concern). (Al Imran 3:159-160)

Mildness toward people initiated by Prophet Abraham reached perfection with Prophet Muhammad.

No Compulsion in Religion

A fundamental rule of Islam is expressed by the Quranic verse, "There is no compulsion in religion" (Baqara 2:256). Because of this rule, Islam is very different from inflexible thought systems and other religious traditions. Indeed it was Prophet Abraham who taught the necessity of this attitude of tolerance and latitude toward other beliefs. For, in his preaching to his people, part of his central message was that "a Prophet's responsibility is only to convey the message." The deeper meaning of this is that "There is no compulsion in religion" and "Prophets are not to force or coerce" (Ghashiya 88:22), and that if others who claim to follow the religion of Abraham have done so, this is an alteration or distortion of the revelation which was given.

Some things are best left to God

One of the most essential messages we can take from Prophet Abraham's life is to, as a rule, fulfill one's duties exactly in the way that it has been commanded, and leave the rest to God. Until the time of his attempted execution by fire, despite all his life's work up to that point, not a single person had believed in Abraham's message. Completely alone, he struggled to defend the truth against an entire society. Even more, he always followed the methods which were best and most suitable for human character and temperament. This was because he acted within the boundaries drawn by the Creator of all things, Who best knows their nature.

Despite all of this, he had not a single follower in all the time preceding his attempted execution. Yet he never fell into despair, and continued his struggle with unflagging energy, because he understood that it was required of Prophets to "convey the message." A Prophet was not to concern himself with what effects his preaching had, or whether people accepted it. After conveying the message, he was to leave the rest to the people and God. If it was God's will, He would allow people to accept guidance and follow the Prophet, increasing their numbers. According to Prophet Muhammad, some prophets had only one or two followers, and others were not believed by even a single person.

If the prophets relied on success that was measured by the size of their following, their missions would have been short-lived indeed. For instance, Prophet Abraham would have lost his enthusiasm long before achieving the success he was eventually granted; perhaps he would have never done the things that brought him to that blazing fire, such as breaking the idols."[28]

Yet he did not think this way; he persevered in carrying out God's commands. Thus he left a timeless legacy to those who struggle in God's way, which will never change until the Judgment Day: working for God's pleasure means never expecting any worldly rewards.

HINTS OF FUTURE TECHNOLOGY

We would like to quote some comments of Said Nursi on the Prophet Abraham and a related verse. Nursi points out previously overlooked messages from Prophet Abraham. He emphasizes that miracles worked by the Prophets might give us an indication about the highest level we can reach by technology. These miracles also relate to our eternal salvation in the Hereafter. He writes as follows:

"The verse: *"'O fire' We ordered, 'Be cool and peaceful for Abraham'"* (Anbiya 21:69), which is about one of Abraham's miracles, contains three subtle indications:

First: Like every element in nature, fire performs a duty under a command. It did not burn Abraham, for God commanded it not to do so.

Second: One type of heat burns through coldness. Through the phrase *Be... peace*, God Almighty ordered the cold: 'Like heat, do not burn him.' It is simultaneously fire and cold. Science has discovered a fire called 'white heat,' which does not radiate its heat. Instead, by attracting the surrounding heat, it causes the surrounding area to become cold enough to freeze liquids and in effect burns them through its cold (Hell, which contains all degrees and sorts of fire, also must have this intense cold).

Third: Just as there is an immaterial substance like belief and armor like Islam, which will remove and protect the effects of Hellfire, there must be a physical substance that will protect against and prevent the effects of fire. As is required by His Name the All-Wise, and since this world is the Abode of Wisdom, [where everything occurs for a definite purpose and usually according to cause and effect], God Almighty acts behind the veil of cause and effect. Therefore, as the fire did not burn Abraham's body or clothes, He gave them a state that resisted fire.

Thus the verse suggests:

> O nation of Abraham. Be like Abraham, so that your garments may be your guard against the fire, your greatest enemy, in both worlds. Coat your spirit with belief, and it will be your armor against Hellfire. Moreover, the earth contains substances that will protect you from fire's evil. Search for them, extract them, and coat yourselves with them.

As an important step in progress, humanity has discovered a fire-resistant substance. But see how elevated, fine, and beautiful a garment this verse indicates, a garment that will be woven on the loom of purity of belief in and submission to God, and which will not be rent for all eternity."[29]

LESSONS FROM THE SUPPLICATIONS OF ABRAHAM

The prayers and supplications found in the Qur'an deserve careful attention as they show what things must be given primary importance in the life of a Muslim. There are different types of prayers, including some that were practiced by the Prophets. The supplications and entreaties of Prophet Abraham can be very instructive.

Although I will later examine several lessons that can be taken from the Prophet Abraham's prayers, I believe it is necessary to first provide a deeper background, that will lead to a better understanding, allowing us to reap greater benefit. After explaining in greater detail why I have mentioned these supplications, I will return to the subject of Abrahamic prayers.

In the Islamic understanding, making supplications is a form of worship, even being called "the soul of worship."[30] The human being, who was created for worship, has a nature and essence that requires first faith and then supplication. When a person entreats God to fulfill his needs, they not only are aware of their servanthood but also their neediness, and in beseeching the Almighty One for these needs, they declare that He alone is powerful. In addition, by saying, "I shall do that which is asked of me" and making supplications, the believer also wins God's pleasure by responding to God's call to come to Him in prayer.

We ask from God with our tongue and we also make requests with our actions. In fact, to completely adhere to Islamic ethics, it is necessary when we say that we want something that it is followed up by an appropriate action. If one asks only with words and then neglects to carry out whatever is necessary to facilitate the requested result, this does not fit into the Islamic concept of prayer. To do so would be to display an erroneous understanding of "reliance" that is actually closer to becoming resignation.

It is a similar type of negligence to engage only in "active" prayer and to avoid actually asking for one's needs. This leads to the misguided stance of seeking what we need from physical or material "causes" rather than from God. "It is an active prayer to farm the land. Our daily bread does not come from the soil. The soil is like a door to God's mercy, and the plow knocks on this door."[31]

In order to avoid doing too much or too little, first ask God for what you need, then do what you can to bring about the necessary conditions—applying to material causes—for it to occur. The Prophet Muhammad told someone who asked whether he should protect his camel from being stolen by praying to God or by tying up his camel, "First, tie up your camel, then pray (for its safety)!" Likewise, Rabia ibn Kab al-Aslami, who begged to be close to God in Paradise, was told "Help yourself (toward this goal) by increasing your prostrations."[32]

Thus, the proper way to pursue requests is to ask God, either verbally or at least by making an intention, and then proceed to bring about all the preparations and causes that seem to us necessary for the request to come about, as much as lies within our reach; leave the rest to God.

When understood this way, it becomes clear that when a supplication is made either verbally or by intention, it is necessary for the supplicant to think consciously about the request and follow this up with an attempt to perform the measures required to bring the desired event about. A person who prays for something but does not work to create the necessary conditions, who does not make an action plan or carry it out, is like a farmer who expects the harvest to appear in his hands without ever touching his plow. Furthermore, gathering in a harvest requires more than plowing; the farmer has to pay attention to many aspects of the process, such as planting, watering, ensuring the right amount of light, and protecting the crops from harm.

Prophet Abraham's prayers show, first of all, that a supplicant must bring their request to God, while at the same time not neglecting their own duties in bringing it about. This is all part of the "message" that is found in his prayers.

MANNERS AND MORALS IN PRAYER

The prayers and supplications of Prophet Abraham contain much more than just a list of things that must be sought from God. They also contain information about what kinds of things a prayer should have if it is to be acceptable. These morals for how to conduct oneself in prayer must be attended to first.

Performing a good deed before prayer: Prophet Abraham and his son Ishmael made supplications after having completed good works as significant as, for example, raising the foundations of the Ka'ba:

> And when Abraham, and Ishmael with him, raised the foundations of the House (they were praying):
>
> "Our Lord! Accept (this service) from us. Surely You are the All-Hearing, the All-Knowing. Our Lord! Make us Muslims, submissive to You, and of our offspring a community Muslim, submissive to You. Show us our rites of worship (including particularly the rites of the Pilgrimage) and accept our repentance (for our inability to worship You as worshipping You requires). Surely You are the One Who accepts repentance and returns it with liberal forgiveness and additional reward, the All-Compassionate. Our Lord! Raise up among that community a Messenger of their own, reciting to them Your Revelations, and instructing them in the Book (that You will reveal to him) and the Wisdom, and purifying them (of false beliefs and doctrines, of sins and all kinds of uncleanness). Surely You are the All-Glorious with irresistible might, the All-Wise." (Baqara 2:127-129)

Repentance and asking forgiveness in prayers: This can be seen in the prayer just cited. Supplications made after cleansing one's soul by repentance are more likely to be granted.

Praying for others and not only for oneself: This too can be clearly seen in the prayer above; it is important to include one's family, friends, and all believers in one's prayers.

Being persistent in prayers: When it is observed how many times Prophet Abraham repeatedly came to God beseeching certain things, it becomes obvious that what made him unique was how often he offered supplications. This suggests that it is not appropriate to pray for something once and think that will be enough. If the thing for which one prays has visible results, then one should continue praying until these are seen; if not—such as with prayers for forgiveness of sins—one must keep asking throughout one's entire life, every day, even every hour if possible.

How to Benefit From Abraham's Prayers

In order to benefit from the prayers of Abraham and the other prayers related in the Qur'an, I would like to call attention to one or two more related points.

1) The Qur'an presents for our consideration the matter of prayer which is critical for a servant (believer), demanding the utmost attention or a careful eye, and teaches us to adhere to the following statements.

2) The prayers in the Qur'an—and especially those of Prophet Abraham—should not only be read and passed by. Those who wish to learn from them should carefully analyze each detail of these prayers, so that they are better able to understand what must be included and avoided in making supplications.

3) Most importantly, to realize these aims, appropriate plans and projects must be formulated by informing our reason and intellect with the form and technique found in these prayers, making an attempt to use all these resources to carry out the measures taught. For instance, take as a model one of his supplications: "O my Lord! Give me a righteous child," he said. We should not take this only literally and wait for our children to just grow up and be righteous. What we need to do is contribute to this prayer with "active prayer." This is such a serious issue in which there are many things to be done from the very beginning on—from being careful from the time of conception about what is eaten by the mother (nothing forbidden by God or earned through unlaw-

ful means should be consumed), to the name we give the child, from what we teach them as they grow up to how we discipline them… Islam has introduced a detailed system of child-raising.

Someone who wishes to take a lesson from Abraham's life will first understand from this that to have a righteous child is a goal of life, and they will then try to determine what is meant by being "righteous" on God's path. Once this is clear, this person will examine the time in which they live to find out what is necessary to reach this goal in their own life. After seeking out the knowledge of how this goal can be attained, they will do everything in their power to accomplish, one by one, the steps that will bring them in reach of the target.

THE PRAYERS OF PROPHET ABRAHAM

FIRST PRAYER

Certainty in faith means knowledge which is not sullied by any doubt. For example, everyone knows with certainty that two times two make four. Prophet Abraham beseeched God for this kind of certainty about how the dead would be raised to life.

> And recall when Abraham said: "My Lord, show me how You will restore life to the dead!" God said: "Why? Do you not believe?" Abraham said: "Yes, but that my heart may be at rest. (Baqara 2:260)

SECOND PRAYER

As we have mentioned above, when Abraham and Ishmael raised the foundations of the Ka'ba, they supplicated God. There are a number of requests in this supplication of the Prophet Abraham:

- The acceptance of good deeds,
- To be a servant fully submitted to God,
- To have as descendants a people who would submit to God,

- To be shown the best ways to worship,
- Forgiveness of sins.

THIRD PRAYER

"My Lord! Grant me true, wise judgment, and join me with the righteous. And grant me a most true and virtuous renown among posterity. And make me one of the inheritors of the Garden of bounty and blessing. And forgive my father, for he is among those who have gone astray. And do not disgrace me on the Day when all people will be raised up to life."(Shuara 26:83-87)

In the verse above Abraham prays for the following:

- Knowledge (including understanding, discernment)
- To be among the good
- To pass on blessings to those who would come after him
- Forgiveness for his father
- To be shielded on the Day of Judgment

FOURTH PRAYER

And (remember) when Abraham prayed: "My Lord! Make this land (Mecca) secure, and preserve me and my children (my sons and their descendants) from ever worshipping idols.

My Lord! They have indeed caused many among humankind to go astray. So, he who follows me is truly of me; while he who disobeys me, surely You are All-Forgiving, All-Compassionate.

Our Lord! I have settled some of my offspring (Ishmael and his descendants) in an uncultivable valley near Your Sacred House, so that, our Lord, they may establish the Prayer; so make the hearts of people incline towards them, and provide them with the produce of earth (by such means as trade), so that they may give thanks (constantly from the heart and in speech, and in action by fulfilling Your commandments).

Our Lord! Surely You know all that we keep secret as well as all that we disclose; nothing whatever, whether it be on earth or in heaven, is hidden from God.

All praise and gratitude are for God, Who has granted me, despite my old age, Ishmael and Isaac. Indeed, my Lord is the Hearer of prayer.

My Lord! Make me one who establishes the Prayer in conformity with its conditions, and (likewise) from my offspring (those who are not wrongdoers), Our Lord, and accept my prayer!

Our Lord! Forgive me, and my parents, and all the believers, on the Day on which the Reckoning will be established. (Abraham 14:35-41)

In the verse above Abraham prays for the following:

- For the safety and protection of the place where one lives (in Abraham's case, this is Mecca),
- For himself and his descendants to be saved from idol worship,
- For his people to love their young,
- For his children to be granted with provisions so that they offer thanks to God,
- For himself and his children to be of those who prostrate in worship,
- For his supplications to be granted,
- For himself, his parents, and all believers to be forgiven at the Last Reckoning.

THE CORE OF THE MESSAGE

Prophet Abraham was a man with many distinguished accomplishments, virtues, and messages. His accomplishments, however, were bestowed upon him. This means the example he showed and the virtues he represented did not flow from his own personality. The origin and template of all the characteristics attributed to him in the Qur'an did not belong to him, but to the Lord of the Worlds. These elevated characteristics came from God, the only Source and Creator, who manifested them in Abraham. That is, Abraham was like a screen or mirror reflecting these divine manifestations. It was

God who chose him and elevated him above all people. Knowing this, when he could not convince his father to join him, while Abraham said that he would pray for his father's forgiveness, he did not neglect to add, "...although I have it not in my power to obtain anything from God on your behalf." Real God-consciousness, real *tawhid*, or true understanding of the oneness of God, is to know with certainty that whatever good we are able to attain comes from God, to know that everything comes from God.

PART FOUR

The Contents of the Prophet
Abraham's Teachings

The Scrolls of Abraham

One of the greatest honors bestowed on Prophet Abraham by God was certainly the revelation of a scripture. He was given a Divine revelation called the Scrolls of Abraham. His duty went beyond just being a messenger confirming the teachings of previous Prophets; he brought a completely renewed moral code and faith system. This revelation, which had critical and remarkable differences from earlier messages, represented a new era in human history, a crucial turning point, and the beginning of a new phase of material and spiritual progress; these were all marked by the bestowal of a new scripture.

What did this revealed text contain?

Doubtless some of its messages were the same as those that came to previous Prophets, such as the fundamentals of faith and worship. However, some were also new, though they would of course be repeated in the Prophetic teachings that came after him. In other words, not only did he abrogate some previous teachings; Prophet Abraham also put into effect certain moral standards and laws for the first time in human history, some of which will remain in effect until the end of time.

Despite our curiosity as to what exactly these were, the incomplete state and questionable authenticity of those parts of the text that remain today make it impossible to know this with certainty. In spite of this, I will outline some of the basic Abrahamic principles mentioned in the Qur'an and *hadith*.[1]

The chapter goes on to mention some specific principles. Some are concerned with the world and some with the Hereafter; some with societal ethics, others with true belief. There are also some basic rights which can be outlined on the basis of the following:

1. No one can suffer punishment for another person's sins (personal responsibility).

2. Nothing will be accounted unto a person but what they are striving for (what they consciously intend).[2]

3. Those who work (may be saved and) will be made successful and given the most perfect reward.

4. Every individual's final return is to their Lord.

5. It is God who causes both laughter and tears (God-consciousness and belief in the Final Judgment are also granted by God.)

6. It is He who gives life and takes life.

7. It is also He who has the power to bring about a second life (resurrection at the end of time).

8. It is God alone who frees human beings from want, and He who enriches and causes them to have possessions.

9. It is He alone who sustains the brightest star.

10. It was He who brought destruction to the ancient tribes of Ad and Thamud.

11. It is also God who brought a similar fate to Noah's people because they were oppressors and aggressors.

12. In the same way it was He who brought down judgment on the people of Lot.[3]

Another Qur'anic verse attributes the following teachings to the Books given to Prophets Abraham and Moses:

1. Happiness in the life to come will indeed be attained by one who attains purity, remembers the Sustainer's name, and prays unto Him.

2. Although some people prefer the worldly life to the life of the Hereafter, the latter is better and more enduring.[4]

Apart from the Qur'an, there is also some information about this book to be found in the *hadiths* of the Prophet Muhammad, peace be upon him. According to Abu Dharr al-Ghifari;

In answer to the question, "O Messenger of God! What was written in the scroll of Abraham?" the Prophet answered, "It was full of parables," and gave examples of some of these:

"O you proud king who is being tested! I did not send you to pile up worldly goods for yourself. I sent you to work for righteousness, to behave with justice, and to put an end to persecution. For I will not suffer the pleas of the oppressed to be turned away, even if they be unbelievers."[5]

The rest of the hadith informs us that those who have wisdom should strive to spend their days in three pursuits:

1. Setting aside time to pray and worship one's Sustainer.
2. Setting aside time to call oneself to account for deeds and to meditate on the correctness of one's actions.
3. Using the remainder of one's time to fulfill one's needs and goals in appropriate and acceptable ways. The time spent in the first two activities helps to prepare the heart and purify intentions for the time spent in the latter way.

A tradition related by Tabari divides the day into four parts. These include the three above as well as time for "contemplation of Creation."[6]

A wise person will not only be judicious and careful with their time, but will also ensure that they control their tongue, for the words of those who speak little are more valuable and worthwhile; such words are counted as good deeds. On this topic, a saying quoted in Tabari is "Whoever realizes his words are deeds will speak less often and say more valuable words."[7]

Wise people are on a journey for three things:

1. To attain that which is necessary for physical life (or as Tabari says, "things that will improve the worldly life").
2. To make preparations and provisions for the Hereafter.
3. To enjoy that which is not forbidden or wrong.[8]

From these traditions it can further be understood that the following messages were brought to humanity by Prophet Abraham:

Because of the importance of justice in social relations, no human being can be persecuted for rejecting belief, even if they oppose believers.

It is very important to use time well by planning one's days.

It is crucial never to neglect to take time out of our business every day for worship, meditation, and spiritual pleasures.

Meaningless, useless pursuits should be avoided.

One should be prepared for the Hereafter at all times.

It is not wrong to enjoy healthy pleasures if one avoids wrongdoing.

PROPHET ABRAHAM'S FAMILY ETHICS

In the Qur'anic verses which are concerned with the Prophet Abraham, a constantly repeated characteristic is his concern for his family. At every opportunity he thought of his family; he took great care for their material and spiritual well being, prayed for them, and provided for them. Indeed the deep devotion with which he approached all who were under his care was implied earlier when we discussed how much he worried about his father and pleaded for his salvation.

His concern for his children was no less than that he showed to his father. Such was his concern that, when he was told that he would receive great blessings, he immediately asked the same for them: "God said, 'I will make you the leader of all people,' and he replied, '(Raise up righteous leaders among) my descendents also!'"

God Almighty did not reject this prayer, but the answer suggests that from Abraham's line would also come oppressors: "My covenant does not include the wrongdoers" (Baqara 2:124).

Likewise, his beseeching God for both worldly and eternal blessings for his family, as seen in his prayers, demonstrates how much the Prophet Abraham took pains to care for them.

It was this keen conscientiousness regarding his family that drove him to attend them with the best possible treatment. Such prayer brings consciousness to every action, making it possible to stay on the right path. Along with prayer, one must do what is necessary to bring about the conditions in which the prayer may be granted; Said Nursi refers to this as "fulfilling the requirement of causes" created by God. Thus the compassion and mercy he felt toward his family meant that their physical and spiritual health were naturally issues that were of paramount importance for the Prophet Abraham. Their worldly comfort and enjoyment was not enough for him; he wanted to ensure their spiritual development and eternal salvation as well. Because of this, Prophet Abraham, out of his profound concern for his family, gave equal importance to their physical and spiritual needs and thus formed for us the basic ideals for how to treat family members.

PRIORITIES IN FAMILY ETHICS

When delving into the topic of etiquette in the family and the correct treatment of family members there are a myriad of details that must be addressed. Doubtless, it is impossible here to go into Prophet Abraham's connection with each and every one. However, I would be remiss not to mention some major points of interest on this issue that are found in the Qur'anic verses concerned with him.

CHOOSING A PLACE FOR THE FAMILY

It is not a coincidence that Prophet Abraham moved his family to the sacred precinct of Mecca. This was just a step, probably the first step, of a conscious plan.[9] Thus I would like to start this section here. In a Qur'anic verse Abraham says, *Our Lord! I have settled some of my offspring in an uncultivable valley near Your Sacred House, so that, our Lord, they may establish the Prayer...*" (Ibrahim 14:37).

First of all, this verse contains three messages:

- One of the most important considerations in caring for a family is making a plan in order to ensure that children can learn about faith.
- The environment where this education is provided is one of the most important things to consider because it has such an influence on the children.
- It is also necessary to think about the economic aspects of the place.

Now we will turn to the verses which mention issues related to establishing a good environment for the family.

Being near a place of worship

Prophet Abraham moved his family close to the House of God, which is first and foremost a place of worship. But at the same time this was a place that made it possible to meet and mix with people who shared the same beliefs, to gather with them for communal worship, and to exchange ideas and cultures, and even to engage in trade. In other words, Mecca was a place that provided an extraordinary wealth of human interaction and all the benefits that go with this.

Since every house of prayer is symbolically seen as the House of God,[10] those who wish to follow in Prophet Abraham's footsteps should take care to raise their families in the shadow of a house of worship—close enough for them to hear the call to prayer.

Economic considerations

The verse seems to link the "convenience of worship" with the fact that Mecca is not arable land. Thus we can conclude that an environment which is not arable brings a lifestyle that is more amenable to devoting oneself to worship. Perhaps fertile soil and green lands detract from one's attention, because of the many pleasures they bring—the fruit, flowers, shade, and the temptation to busy ourselves with gardening and tillage.

Firstly it must be understood that this does not mean Islam is opposed to agriculture. In fact, there are *hadith* and verses that encourage farming. On the other hand, the message here seems to be calling attention to a human weakness in which there are some risks associated with the work of tillage. It is a warning that in such circumstances people are more inclined to neglect the development of their consciousness. Here it is relevant to point out the following:

- In the Qur'an the Prophet Adam's first son, whose sacrifice was accepted by God, was a "pious" shepherd (Maida 5:28), while his brother, whose sacrifice was not accepted and who became the first murderer, was a farmer.[11]
- Again in the Qur'an, the story is told of a very wealthy man who owned many date trees and vineyards full of every kind of grape; his wealth made him heedless and ungrateful before God, so much so that even the advice of his friends made no difference, and he lost all that he had (Qaf 50:32-34).
- Similarly, in chapter 68, the detailed story of the plantation owners who perished vividly portrays the errors in thought and behavior that such owners can fall into.
- Likewise, the ancient people of Sheba, who fell into perdition (Saba 34:15-17), were a nation very advanced in agricultural expertise.
- The dwellers of Ayka can be given as another example (Shuara 26:176). The word *ayka* itself means a "thick grove of trees."[12]

Considering all these examples, it can be said that agriculture—compared to other professions—is more likely to have a role in negatively influencing a person's ability to remain pious and humble.

This careful attention to the importance of one's surroundings so that one can better follow and carry out God's commands is one of the messages of Abraham's life for those who wish to follow him. It should be emphasized again that it would be erroneous to assume that this means the Qur'an is somehow opposed to agriculture and farming. Instead, it warns those who cultivate the land

and alerts them to the temptation which can make them forget to work for the Hereafter as well. Nevertheless, to fully understand the point of all these prophetic and Qur'anic indications, I would like to add this observation about human history: Particularly in our day, countries that rely economically on agriculture are under-developed, and their people are relatively poor. Those who are advanced in heavy industry are more successful in trade. We can understand the Abrahamic message here to be, "Do not be so blinded by the appeal of the flowers and harvest of tillage that you fail to recognize the importance of knowledge, cultural exchange, and the technological advancement it brings to civilization." This interpretation is more correct and also more relevant to our purpose.

In actuality, the huge impact of environment on moral education is well known. I will not go into detail here, but will simply offer a few quotes from sociology:

"An individual's social characteristics are owed not to the training received at school, but to the circumstances of the setting... Culture is related much more to the environment than to formal education....the setting determines the cultural values... schooling is one element of culture, but to think that it can solve cultural problems would be a misrepresentation of its function."[13]

Hence, Prophet Abraham moved his family to the place he believed would be the most conducive to their ability to worship.

Safe surroundings

The Prophet Abraham's another important consideration was that the place be safe. For he had prayed in this place, "O my Sustainer, make this land secure!" (Ibrahim 14:35). As a matter of fact, to develop every part of a person's being—both physically and spiritually—an individual needs personal security as much as they need clothing, nourishment, and companionship. If a person lives in danger of losing the security or freedom of their possessions, their life, honor, beliefs, and intellectual life, they cannot reach their full potential. It is for this reason that the Prophet Abraham made a safe homeland his first priority for those he loved and for those who followed him. For Muslims, a place where their worship, fasting, abstention from alcohol, choice of modest clothing, etc. bring persecution is not a secure place to live.

Social milieu

After relating how Prophet Abraham moved his family to the place most amenable to worship, the same verse goes on to say that he asked God for a loving and positive social environment for them: "Our Sustainer, cause people's hearts to incline towards them..."

From this we understand that one of the characteristics of an ideal milieu—indeed, one of the most important ones—is to be part of a community where one is embraced. Moreover, some *hadith* suggest that believers should live in secure places in order to avoid any hindrance in observing Islam or any other negative outcomes.[14]

SUPPORTING ONE'S FAMILY

In addition to their social milieu, Prophet Abraham also thought about his family's sustenance: "Our Lord! ... so make the hearts of people incline towards them, and provide them with the produce of the earth (by such ways as trade), so that they may give constant thanks (from the heart, verbally, and by fulfilling Your commandments)" (Ibrahim 14:37). Indeed, he asked for them to be nourished with "fruitful sustenance" although his family lived in a place that was not suitable for growing crops. This means the economy of this place must have been so sound that, despite not having any farms, the people there were able to eat the same fruit and crops raised in places that were agriculturally rich. This request should be taken as a guidance that encourages the use of the strategies necessary for the development of economic means to reach such a condition. Indeed, it is made plain in the chapter Quraysh that the people of Mecca were very well fed all year round through thriving trade.

AWARENESS OF THE RELIGION

Notably, such an approach also shows that provisions are given by God and therefore the recipient should be thankful. Every kind of blessing is bestowed so that the servant will be grateful. A believer knows that the reason for their creation and the purpose of life is to serve God. Thus, all material things that are needed to continue life are purely occasions for thankfulness, not for pleasure and enjoyment or for gratifying the ego. Indeed, just as God declares that humans and the jinn were created only for worship, and that He does not want food from us,[15] and admonishes all people who put other things before worship.[16] Yet another verse[17] exhorts us to remember God when standing up, sitting, and lying down. In one sense, this indicates that ideally, in all activities, a person should remember God. This does not mean spending every moment only in worship, but rather doing all that one does in a worshipful manner. In other words, by completing the prescribed prayers and worship, avoiding that which is not permissible, and following the way of the prophets, all our daily actions—including sleep, relaxation, conversation, and legitimate cultural traditions—will be counted as worship; this is confirmed both by the *hadith* and the explanations of religious scholars. The Prophet Abraham's moving his family to a better social milieu at a crucial stage of their development reminds us that gratefulness to the Sustainer should be the motivation for whatever we do. This certainly contains an important lesson for today. There may be those who find this Abrahamic message odd at a time when such considerations have given way to completely materialistic concerns. To such people, who do not think of the long-term development of their families, I would like to point out that corrupt actions are now seen every day.

To recap what has been said so far: this Abrahamic message invites us to plan carefully for the life of the next generation, preparing them for service to God.

Priority of prescribed prayers

In continuation of the above-mentioned Qur'anic passage, which discusses the decision of Prophet Abraham to move his family to an inhospitable land so that they could better worship, we see him listing and praising some of the attributes of God, and then petitioning for obedience as the first priority both for himself and his posterity:

> My Lord! Make me one who establishes the Prayer in conformity with its conditions, and (likewise) from my offspring (those who are not wrongdoers), Our Lord, and accept my prayer! (Ibrahim 14:40)

The matters we have touched on show that in all the Prophet Abraham's actions and measures, faith in God Almighty and obedience were central. This is the reason he was honored with the exalted station of "Friendship" to God. Here I would like to point out that it is a Qur'anic imperative that precedence be given to teaching the prescribed prayers when educating one's family. This directive was given to the Prophet Muhammad: "Order your family and community to establish the Prayer, and be diligent in its observance. We do not ask you to provide for Us; rather it is We Who provide for you (o all your worship is for your own benefit)" (Ta Ha s20:132).

The Prophet Muhammad, just like the Prophet Abraham, gave prescribed prayers a place of supreme importance in religion, listing it as one of the "pillars."[18]

Prophet Abraham and his son Ishmael, after reconstructing the Ka'ba according to the commands of God, prayed that they and those who would come from their lineage and heritage would be sincerely obedient:

> Another time, when Abraham, with Ishmael, placed the foundations of the House, praying: "Our Lord! Accept (this service) from us. Surely, You are the All-Hearing, the All-Knowing. Our Lord! Make us Muslims, perfectly submissive to You, and of our offspring a Muslim community, perfectly submissive to You. Show us the ways in which we must worship You, (including in particular how we must perform the duty of pilgrimage,)

and accept our repentance (for our inability to worship You as worshipping You requires.) Surely, You are the One Who truly returns repentance with liberal forgiveness and extra reward, the All-Compassionate (especially towards His believing servants.) Our Lord! Raise up among that community a Messenger of their own, reciting to them Your Revelations, and instructing them in the Book (You will send to him) and the Wisdom, and purifying them (of false beliefs and doctrines, and sins, and all kinds of filth.) Surely, You are the All-Honored with irresistible might, the All-Wise." (Baqara 2:127-129)

Prophet Abraham prayed the best prayer that a compassionate and concerned parent can pray on behalf of his children and all his descendants, even to the Last Day: praying not for their material prosperity, but for their success in the prescribed prayers and all other good deeds on the path of servanthood to God. Thus he established and taught by example the need for believers to take responsibility for trying to impart this to coming generations, and pleaded for these things on their behalf.

SUPPLICATION FOR FORGIVENESS

Obedience includes much more than observing the prescribed prayers. Those who wish to draw close to God and attain eternal salvation through true servanthood must not only pray and worship faithfully, but they also must avoid falling into error. In fact, in a *hadith* it is stated that no one can "deserve" to be admitted to Paradise through their own deeds, including the prophets, as this depends solely on the mercy and forgiveness of God. Therefore we can say that it is advisable for one who prays for being observant of the prayers to ask forgiveness also, which is complementary to them. We learn from the Qur'an that this is how the Prophet Abraham prayed. One of the prayers most often offered by Muslims has come to us from him:

Our Lord! Forgive me, and my parents, and all the believers, on the Day on which the Reckoning will be established. (Ibrahim 14:41)

According to one narration from Prophet Muhammad, on the Day of Judgment Prophet Abraham will see his father and will once again appeal to God's mercy, "O my Lord! You promised me that when you resurrected me nothing would make me disconsolate; can there be a greater disconsolation than that my father should be kept from Your mercy?" This appeal will not be accepted by God, who will say, "I have forbidden Heaven to the unbelievers."[19]

In this hadith there are two important Abrahamic messages:

1. Family ties are strong and serious bonds. However much one works for and shows ardor for the eternal salvation of those close to them, it will never be too much. The Prophet Abraham, whose zeal for his father's soul will extend even to the Hereafter, exemplifies this.

2. Faith comes before everything and unbelief severs all ties. Even the Prophet Abraham, one of the greatest prophets, cannot intercede for his father since intercession cannot save an unbelieving person.

Therefore, the believers, who wish to attain salvation on the Abrahamic path need to take the criterion of supporting faith and opposing unbelief in balancing their personal relationships.

HIGH PROFESSIONAL IDEALS

Presumably, when educating his children, Prophet Abraham did not stop merely at praying that they would be people of belief[20] and worship or that they would be among the righteous.[21] He also must have taken care to help them in their worldly living and occupation. The best clue on this issue is that when God said to him, "I will make you a leader to the nations," his response was to request the same for people from his descendants. In a way, this is related to the fulfillment of worldly goals. Prophet Abraham is asking that his children will be leaders of their people. When leadership was given to him, he wanted it for his children also. And this request was realized: From his line came several prophets, the most brilliant jewels of humanity—Ishmael, Isaac, Jacob, Moses, and so on down to Jesus and Muhammad (peace and blessings be upon all of them).

Accordingly, this prayer is a meaningful message: "We must think of our children's professional lives, and guide them toward the most ideal, esteemed, and praiseworthy occupational pursuits."[22] This Abrahamic principle could also be the underlying rationale for the ruling by Islamic scholars that it is not correct for a father to prepare his child for an occupation less well-esteemed than his own.

Even today, in popular opinion the highest professional achievement is leadership, in the form of presidency or similar political offices.

EDUCATIONAL GUIDANCE

Prophet Abraham's relationship to his family as a father is not one of the best-known aspects of his life. Several traditions say that he took his wife Hagar and his son Ishmael to the desert and left them to live there, occasionally visiting them. Nevertheless, as I previously pointed out, there are some details in one narration on this subject, which states that he left them in Mecca and subsequently came to see them three times.

Though not perfectly authenticated, some of these narrations mention that Prophet Abraham visited Hagar and Ishmael on a monthly basis. Ibn Hajar quotes the following from Abu Jahm: "Prophet Abraham rode the Buraq (holy steed) to Mecca and visited Hagar once a month, arriving in the morning and miraculously returning to his home in Damascus for the customary noontime rest." Ibn Hajar also reports another narration in Faqihi, in which Ali is said to have related a similar story.[23]

It seems credible that Prophet Abraham, whose life was overflowing with excellence, could have visited his family each month as an example to his followers and as part of his legacy. It should not be regarded as strange that he was rewarded with God's pleasure for such actions, and it behooves us to assume from his character that all his actions were the best; otherwise there would be no satisfactory explanation for the perfect obedience and submission shown even at such a young age by his son Ishmael, as the sacrifice story demonstrates.

Thus, while the daily care of Prophet Muhammad for his family is the ideal, the monthly visits of Prophet Abraham demonstrate the maximum time that is acceptable for parents to be away from their offspring. Those with children who still need parental education would do well to follow this Abrahamic example as a basic principle, and not to unnecessarily extend any periods of separation. If something such as illness is expected to cause such a separation, at the very least precautions must be taken, as much as is possible, to avoid any harm it may cause the child; in other words, it is crucial to be consciously vigilant about the effects of separation on the child.

Abraham's will to his children

The Prophet Abraham also left an excellent example in terms of the leader of a family taking responsibility for the development of other members of the family. He paid close attention to all the measures necessary for ensuring that his family would stay on the Straight Path in their faith for the remainder of their lives.

It is not enough to find a suitable location for one's family, although this is one of the primary considerations. Throughout their development, continual admonitions and reminders, counsel and supervision are needed.

> Abraham willed this submission to his sons (Ishmael and Isaac) and (to his grandson) Jacob, saying: "My sons, (out of different ways of faith and life,) God has chosen for you the religion (of Islam based on submission to Him and absolutely free from associating any kind of partners with Him). See that you die only as Muslims (who have submitted to Him). (Baqara 2:132)

Thus Prophet Abraham exhorted his family to accept, as he himself had done, the command of God to "surrender." His own response is related in the verse immediately prior:

"I have surrendered myself unto [You,] the Sustainer of all the worlds." (Baqara 2:131)

This exhortation to his children to "surrender to the Lord of the Worlds" is followed directly by a section about the Prophet Jacob, which clarifies the nature of his exhortation: staying on the Straight Path of Islam until death. These verses should be looked at with this in mind:

When his Lord told him, "Submit yourself wholly (to your Lord)," he responded: "I have submitted myself wholly to the Lord of the Worlds." Abraham willed this submission to his sons (Ishmael and Isaac) and (to his grandson) Jacob, saying: "My sons, (out of different ways of faith and life,) God has chosen for you the religion (of Islam based on submission to Him and absolutely free from associating any kind of partners with Him.) See that you die only as Muslims (who have submitted to Him (Despite this, and as Children of Jacob—Israel—claiming faithfulness to him, you refuse to enter Islam.) Or were you witnesses when death came to Jacob (that you claim that he made a will other than the one that Abraham wrote? Whereas,) and he asked his sons, "What will you worship after me?" They answered: "We will worship your God and the God of your fathers, Abraham, Ishmael, and Isaac, the One God; we are Muslims who have submitted to Him." (Baqara 2:131-133)

In other words, the duty to educate one's family is not particular to just one context and time in the past, rather it continues "from the cradle to the grave." The most crucial period is until the children's adolescence and the head of a family must answer to God on this issue.[24]

Sacrificing his son

When discussing the blessings and benefits that can be personally reaped from the concern Prophet Abraham had for those who would come after him, the story of the sacrifice of his son must be the most striking, unforgettable, meaningful, and the most profitable as a lesson, as well as being the most emotionally touching message of the rich heritage he left to his descendants and all who came from his line; this is true for us as well, as we are among those included in his prayers. God Himself called this experience a "trial, clear in itself."[25]

Probably to reinforce the lesson and the message that we can gain from this occasion, the Qur'an speaks in other places about the tender affection Prophet Abraham bore for his family, going into more detail. If we were told about a father who did not care much about his family, the lesson to be taken from such a father's obedience to the order would not be emphasized as much as that of Abraham's.

The Prophet Abraham prayed and beseeched for a son and he was granted this precious blessing in his old age, and then he received the sign to sacrifice him. The fact that he obeyed the command to sacrifice this beloved son without the slightest hesitation helps us better understand why his complete submission to God and his sincere obedience are praised in the Qur'an. In light of this test and measure of his character, the message he brought can be better appreciated and understood. The Qur'an tells us the following story:

> And he prayed: "My Lord, Grant me the gift of a child who will be one of the righteous. So We gave him the glad tiding of a boy (to grow as one), mild and forbearing. Then, when he (the son) reached in his company the age of striving for the necessities of life, he (Abraham) said: "O my dear son! I have seen in my dream (for the last few nights) that I should offer you in sacrifice. So think about this and tell me your view!" The son answered unhesitatingly: "O my dear father! Do as you are commanded. You will find me, by God's will and leave, one of those who show good patience in obeying God's commands. So both submitted to God's will, and Abraham laid him down on the side of his forehead. And, just at that time, We called out to him: "O Abraham! You have fulfilled what is required by loyalty to (the order you received in) the dream; (so you no longer have to offer your son in sacrifice). Thus do We reward those devoted to doing good being ever conscious that God sees them." Behold, all this was indeed a trial, clear in itself. And We ransomed him with a sacrifice tremendous in worth And We

> left him thus to be remembered and to live with his Message among later generations (to come until the end of time). Greeting with peace, thanks, and good reputation to Abraham. Thus do We reward those devoted to doing good, being ever conscious that God always sees them. Surely he was one of Our truly believing servants. (Saffat 37:100-111)

Here it would be appropriate to repeat one more time that almost all the divine blessings granted to Prophet Abraham were given him as rewards after successfully passing various kinds of tests; he was able to do this by using his will, and it was this which pleased God.

THE APPROPRIATE FORM OF MERCY

If we look at the aspects of the Abrahamic family ethic that have been described so far, we will see that all of them share one thing: Abraham did not focus solely on their material comfort and provision for the future; on the contrary, he looked to both their physical and spiritual well being.

He educated them with the central tenet of learning to work toward submitting to God and pleasing Him, emphasizing that other things must be sacrificed in order to follow this path.

In this Abrahamic example we can see the steps and preventive measures that must be taken by someone who truly undertakes to carry this burden, in response to the divine admonishment: "Assuredly, the true losers are those who will ruin their own selves and their families on the Day of Resurrection."[26] This is the most beneficial blessing a family can impart to its children; to do so is to do what a truly complete compassion toward them demands. In this way one is able to ensure both their worldly and eternal happiness. To do the opposite—to center our concerns for our family around their material comfort and worldly future—is to misuse and abuse our natural compassion; in other words, it is to take the tools and weapons provided for procuring happiness in both the world and the Hereafter and to use these instead to drive them towards eternal death, as well as bringing down on ourselves the eternal "loss" that is the recompense for this betrayal of our duty to them.

There is no ox that can carry the world on its horns. But mothers and fathers bear a yoke of responsibility so heavy that, were it a stone, it would break the ox's back: the education and raising of the next generation. The responsibility is weighty indeed, but the reward is accordingly generous. While Paradise is not without cost, neither is the Hell created in vain.

HARMONY WITH A SPOUSE

One aspect of the stories about Prophet Abraham's life is worth mentioning here, even though it is not mentioned in the Qur'an: his deeply considerate treatment of his first wife Sarah. As several traditions relate, Sarah arranged for her servant Hagar—who had been a gift to her from the Pharaoh —to marry her husband in the hopes that their union would produce a child to gladden Abraham's heart. And Prophet Abraham did become a father, through this second marriage, to Prophet Ishmael.

After Prophet Ishmael was born, however, Sarah began to feel jealous of Hagar and became very uneasy. She requested that her husband not live in the same place with Hagar, but rather remove her to a place far away from them. Prophet Abraham, whose loyalty the Qu'ran confirms and praises,[27] was naturally not going to refuse Sarah's heartfelt wish. Was it not Sarah who had given Hagar to him in the first place, saying "now you can be a father"? Surely he could not forget this good turn—the more so because it was a sacrifice on Sarah's part. Prophet Abraham, to bring about Sarah's wish and also to fulfill the divine command he had received,[28] took Hagar and baby Ishmael to the place in the desert which is now known as Mecca, being shown this place by divine guidance. Further proof of the loyalty and consideration that Prophet Abraham showed his wife Sarah comes to light when we notice that, before going to visit his wife Hagar and his son Ishmael, he asked Sarah's permission. Sarah agreed, on one condition: that he "go and see them, but return without staying there."[29] This is a suitable place to clarify that in these episodes Sarah's behavior is as worthy of emulation. In order that her husband could have a child, she urged him to marry her servant Hagar. When one considers how difficult this burden would be for a woman in her position, it becomes clear how great a sacrifice this was. Perhaps it was because of this virtuous act that God granted Isaac to her, although she was already 90 years old. Hagar too, is a great example of faithfulness in that she accepted moving to the frightening, empty desert with her baby; she knew that this was the command of God. This action of hers will be discussed in greater depth later on.

GUIDANCE FOR HIS SON IN FAMILY MATTERS

Another area where Prophet Abraham's example should be taken is the way he guided his son Ishmael in regard to his marriage. Elders who have life experience and who are perceptive enough to understand what the future may bring should find a suitable way to share this experience and these perceptions with those around them, so that they too may benefit. We can see this dynamic in the way Prophet Abraham assisted Ishmael in family matters.

The Prophet Abraham found on one of his trips to visit his second family in Mecca that his wife Hagar had died and his son had married; on learning this, he found out where his son lived and went straight to his home. However, when Ishmael's wife came to the door, he found her harsh and crude;[30] when he asked "Are you going to offer me anything to eat?" she responded to him impertinently instead of being courteous to her guest. She said "No, there is no one home!"[31] What is more, he had to listen to her complaints regarding personal, private family matters, which further upset him. When he departed, he found a suitable way to let his son know how unhappy he was by leaving him a coded message. He told the wife, "When your husband returns, tell him that such and such an elder came, and that I say to him, 'I do not like your doorstep—change it.'"

When Ishmael returned his wife told him that an old man had come, described him, and related his message. He realized that it was his father, and that the message meant he should divorce the woman. He said, "That was my father, and you are my doorstep," then divorced her and married another woman.

The next time Prophet Abraham returned to Mecca, again with permission from Sarah to visit only "without staying," he again discovered that his son was not at home. But the new bride was kind and obliging, saying, "My husband has gone hunting; please come in, and hopefully he will return soon!" When he asked, "Do you have anything to offer to me?" She responded in the affirmative. The woman immediately brought milk and meat. Prophet Abraham, happy for his son, prayed for their home to be blessed with plenty. The wife also said, "Let me pour water over your head to refresh you"; Abraham accepted her offer but did not dismount from his steed. She brought the water and also a stone for his feet. She poured the water so he could wash first the right side of his head, by putting his right foot and leaving his footprint on the stone, then the left side in the same way.

Prophet Abraham was pleased by these courteous actions. Then he said to the woman,

"When your husband comes, give him my greeting and tell him such and such an elder came, and that I say to him, 'Your doorstep is good; you should keep it.'"[32] Here the question may be asked: Was the first woman's fault really worthy of divorce?

In the time of Prophet Abraham, it could be. Prophet Muhammad taught that divorce should be avoided and described it as "allowable but disliked by God," advising spouses not to seek divorce for annoying faults but rather to try to live patiently with each other. However, from another perspective, we can say that in this story there is an Abrahamic message that to have a happy marriage it is important to avoid telling family secrets to others, and to cordially greet and patiently attend to anyone who may come to the door as a guest of the family.

MODERATION IN FAMILY AFFECTION

Just as we find among the messages of Abraham a necessary concern for the salvation of one's family, we also find examples for those following his path as to how to avoid typical pitfalls of excess in family matters.

Indeed, in guiding his family, Abraham also exerted himself to try to bring his father to guidance, telling him he was on the wrong path and finding persuasive ways to explain this, but did not get the desired result. Despite the fact his father remained an unbeliever, he said, "I most surely will for you God's forgiveness,"[33] and prayed for his forgiveness: "And forgive my father—for, verily, he is among those who have gone astray."[34]

The Qur'an makes it clear that in these prayers Prophet Abraham is not giving an example to follow: The verse which begins "In Abraham and those with him there is for you a good example," goes on to list some of his exemplary actions, but then says:

> Indeed, you have had a good example in Abraham and those who followed him... the only exception was Abraham's saying to his father, "I most surely will for you God's forgiveness..." (Mumtahana 60:4)

The Qur'an clearly commands that we should not pray for forgiveness for anyone—even a relative—who openly opposes faith. Based on the importance of the issue, in the verse following this command, the Prophet Abraham's prayer for his disbelieving father serves as an example of what *not* to do; and explains that he gave up after learning that there was no hope for his father to believe:

> It is not for the Prophet and those who believe to ask God for the forgiveness of those who associate partners with God even though they be near of kin, after it has become clear to them that they (died polytheists and therefore) are condemned to the Blazing Flame. The prayer of Abraham for the forgiveness of his father was only because of a promise which he had made to him. But when it became clear to him that he was an enemy of God, he (Abraham) dissociated himself from him. Abraham was most tender-hearted, most clement. (Tawba 9:113-114)

In the section about the mercy of the Prophet Abraham, we also saw that because of his gentleness and lenience he pleaded with the angels sent to visit destruction on Lot's people. In this verse too, it explains that when he prayed for his father he was told that he must no longer do so since his father's disbelief and rejection had been confirmed and would not change. The verse then again draws our attention to his being "most tender-hearted and most clement." Thus, the verse brings to the fore another Abrahamic message; despite his gentleness, he had to give up praying for his father since the latter was an enemy of God: "Do not act heedlessly regarding unbelievers—even if they be your own father."

According to the Qur'an this applies to anyone known to be a hypocrite, and it forbids praying for them or visiting their graves: "And never do the funeral Prayer over any of them who dies, nor stand by his grave to pray for him. They surely disbelieved in God and His Messenger and died transgressors."[35]

This Abrahamic message also contains a solution for racism, one of the illnesses of our day. The Qur'an shows the Abrahamic solution in that, far from siding with his own kith and kin against others, he denounced even his own father because of unbelief.

The verses in the Qur'an which dwell on Prophet Abraham's deep concern for his family's guidance must be considered in the light of those verses which repeatedly make it clear that he could not stay tied to his unbelieving father. These verses aim to warn believers against blood feuds, unjust exclusiveness, oppression, bigotry, etc. which can arise from excessive love for one's family and lineage. The critical importance of this Abrahamic message and the reason the Qur'an reiterates this message become all the clearer when we consider those societal ills that result from overly patriotic and/or clannish tendencies.

Abraham's Family and Submission to God

In the same way that Prophet Abraham was a man who thought deeply about preparing a good future for his family, they for their part represent an ideal family that surrounded and supported him. Many of the tests he had to go through in attempting to gain God's pleasure were tests that involved his family.

Were it not for obeying God's command, what normal, sane person, would leave his wife and small baby in the desert where no food, water, or provisions could be found, relying on God for their future and trusting the hidden divine wisdom in such an act? It should, under normal circumstances, be all the more impossible for Prophet Abraham, who embodied the very highest degree of all the merciful qualities a human can have. But since it was a command of God, this servant, whose will was committed to submit to the Lord of All Worlds, carried it out. In addition to the message that God's command must be followed, even if it does not appeal to our reason or judgment, and that in the end this will work out for our good, what other messages can be taken from this? In this vignette, in Abraham's goodbye to Hagar and her baby, are some remarkable lessons that go beyond the classic demonstration of Abraham's supreme virtue.

The willingness of the mother to submit to the decree of God is equally apparent, and in many ways. When her husband took Hagar and her baby Ishmael into an unpopulated desert and was about to return to Damascus, she asked,

"To whom are you leaving us in this dry, empty place?"

She got no answer. How could Prophet Abraham explain this situation, which was a matter solely of submitting, and was not open to human understanding and justifications? How could he tell his wife, who was holding their baby and waiting for his answer, what he felt inwardly? All he could do was remain silent. She asked again and again, but as he did not respond, that exalted lady asked,

"Did God command you to do this?"

Although her question was directed to Prophet Abraham, the woman had been shown the truth, and she understood the answer already.

He answered with a simple "Yes," and Hagar summoned her courageous will to submit to God:

"Then God will not let us be lost!"[36]

This comforted the heart of Abraham, enabling him to continue on his way in peace, without looking back, to continue to obey God's will.

The consent of Hagar that is related in these narratives shows a basic principle that she applied in many difficult circumstances. We will later examine the events surrounding the sacrifice of Ishmael, which deeply affected her.

Those who, in such circumstances, take God's pleasure as their fundamental goal and follow it as a basis for all their decisions—rather than following their ego, base desires, or emotions—will certainly be exalted and held up as examples.

Abraham did not act like a dictator in his family. When he received the directive in a dream, he talked about it with Ishmael, who was old enough to respond, and asked him what he thought about this most serious of questions:

"O my dear son! I have seen in my dream (for the last few nights) that I should offer you in sacrifice. So think about this and tell me your view!"

In this dialogue, when Abraham sincerely sought his son's input, Ishmael chose obedience to God, showing how mature he was and demonstrating that his desire to serve God was truly exemplary—truly worthy of the son of such a father. "O my dear father! Do as you are commanded. You will find me, by God's will and leave, one of those who show good patience in obeying God's commands!" (Saffat 37:102).

In some narrations, the dialogue goes further than in the verse, and these words pour forth from Prophet Ishmael's mouth: "Oh father! If you are to sacrifice me, tie me up so that I may not struggle and reduce my reward. It is not easy to give up my life; I am afraid that when death bears down on me I may resist. Let the blade be sharp so that I will die quickly and not suffer torment. When you lay me down to sacrifice, lay me face down, so that you will not see my face; otherwise your compassion may prevent you from fulfilling God's command. You must bring the knife from behind me so that I won't see it and tremble.[37] Give my shirt to my mother that she may be comforted." Prophet Abraham praised the merit in his requests:

"Oh my son! How helpful you are in assisting me to carry out God's command!"[38]

There are some Qur'anic clues about this conversation that are recorded in the narrations. In the verse immediately following the one we discussed, more details are given about the story, which confirm the obedience shown by the narrations:

> So both submitted to God's will, and Abraham laid him down on the side of his forehead. And, just at that time, We called out to him: "O Abraham! You have fulfilled what is required by loyalty to (the order you received in) the dream; (so you no longer have to offer your son in sacrifice). Thus do We reward those devoted to doing good being ever conscious that God sees them. (Saffat 37:103-105)

And the mother? The Qur'an does not speak of her demeanor in this situation, but the same Abrahamic surrender to God must have been her response as a member of this most blessed family.[39] Despite the details of certain narrations included in some history books, it cannot be said that Prophet Abraham—who took utmost care that his family be provided for in every respect—could have somehow ignored Ishmael's mother in such a serious decision, and taken him for sacrifice secretly if it had been against her wishes. The mother of this graced and blessed family of Abraham, whose heart must have burned ten times more than his at the idea of losing their son, accepted this as the will of God, just as she had accepted being left alone in the desert with the child when he was still a baby. Indeed, a narration of Tabari elaborates on the basic story found in the Qur'an. When Satan attempted to break the mother's resolve by questioning what Abraham was about to do, she answered: "If this is his Sustainer's command, I am submitted to the command of God."[40] According to this narration, Satan came to Prophet Abraham, Prophet Ishmael, and Hagar each in turn to try to cause them to turn away from their duty by playing on their feelings. But each in turn replied, "If God has commanded it, let it be done!"[41]

To sum up, the ideal family; Abraham's family—father, mother, and child—was surrendered to God in everything. As in their individual lives, their family life too honored this first principle of the Islamic Way, surrender to God. Their other qualities and behaviors spring from and flesh out this principle.

In that their hearts had pleased their Sustainer by thus surrendering to Him, this fortunate family, who had mastered their wills, was elevated as an example for all believers until the end of time by the Almighty Creator. This honor outshines even Prophet Abraham's deliverance from the fire, Ishmael's from the knife, and Hagar's from thirst in the desert.

The family of Abraham, who were purified of all evil, are remembered in the prayers of Muslims until the Last Day at least five times daily.

PART FIVE

The Prophet Abraham's
Exemplary Struggle

As we have seen in previous chapters, the Qur'an presents Prophet Abraham with his methods and actions in various circumstances- which we have explored in terms of "messages"- as an exemplar and model to be followed until the end of time. This point is even more evident in his struggle against unbelievers.

Indeed, as mentioned earlier, chapter Mumtahana in the Qur'an, which begins *O you who believe! Do not take My enemies and your enemies for friends...* and establishes principles on how Muslims should treat rejecters of God, mentions Abraham as an exemplar after a half-page of directions and teachings on how to deal with the rejecters:

> Indeed you have had an excellent example to follow in Abraham and those in his company, when they said to their (idolatrous) people (who were their kin): "We are quit of you and whatever you worship besides God. We have rejected you (in your polytheism), and there has arisen between us and you enmity and hate forever until you believe in God alone...." (Mumtahana 60:4)[1]

In examining the verses in the Qur'an regarding Abraham's methodology in his struggle, the long section in Chapter Ankabut (verses 16-27) attracts our attention. This passage summarizes the content of the message to which he invited his people, the evidence and proofs he employed in convincing his audience, his people's reaction against him, etc. The two-page section begins: *And Abraham, too, (We sent as Messenger). He said to his people (in conveying this message): "Worship God alone and keep from disobedience to Him in reverence for Him and piety. Doing so is the best for you, if you would know (the truth of the matter)* (Ankabut 29:16). In the remainder of this passage the following issues are mentioned:

1. The falsity of idol-worship;
2. God has all the power to provide for His creatures, not idols or any other things deified by unbelievers;
3. The final return is to God, and people must serve Him;
4. Warning against denying the Prophets- previous tribes denied their prophets and were destroyed;
5. A Prophet may only invite, he does not force;
6. As careful examination of the world shows, God creates everything;
7. God is Almighty, is not in need of His creatures, and cannot be overpowered;
8. God is the true companion;
9. Rejecters will be deprived of God's mercy.

Upon hearing this Abrahamic invitation, his people reacted by calling for his execution or death by fire. As we know, the decision was to throw him into the fire.

The details of this attempted execution by fire are returned to in later passages of the Qur'an.[1] The section in Chapter Ankabut that is under discussion summarizes stages of Abraham's life, and mentions that Lot believed in him and that Abraham left his people to immigrate to another place.[2]

Thus this section summarizes not only the content of his teaching but also the major stages of his mission. It is possible to find out further details about Abraham's struggle through the explicit and implicit meanings of other Qur'anic verses about him:

– The beginning of his struggle,
– The development of his struggle,
– The initial invitation and teaching,
– Subject matter of the initial invitation,
– Subsequent stages and subjects in his teaching,

In this context I will now go into the most pertinent of these issues under the subtitles gradualness and content.

METHOD OF GRADUALNESS

All the Prophets who have invited people to God's message have always followed a method of gradualness in terms of their audience, the content of their message and even their communication style. This is only natural. Indeed, this is quite evident in the life of Prophet Muhammad: Starting with himself, once he was given Prophethood, he directed his invitation first to his close relatives, then to the area around Mecca, and eventually to all humanity.

In the same manner, his teachings dealt first with issues of faith, then with issues regarding society and religious practice—especially as the community became established in Medina, and there too in a certain sequence. This is clearly visible in detail in the life of Prophet Muhammad. The cornerstones of these stages are even established through revelation in the Qur'an.

Certainly all the Prophets, including Abraham, followed the same principles in their teaching and practiced gradualness. However, in the case of Abraham we are unable to provide as many details as we can for Prophet Muhammad, due to lack of information and questionable reliability of some existing information.

We should note that despite all this, the details about his audience and methods are richer than those regarding the content of his message. In order to discover the Abrahamic messages that are significant for us, we will endeavor to explore the existing information under two subtitles: gradualness in audience and gradualness in the content.

GRADUALNESS IN AUDIENCE

The Qur'anic evidence for the order in which Abraham addressed different audiences during his Prophethood is not as numerous as that regarding Prophet Muhammad.

Still, there are indications which allow a rough chronology of his mission to be established without much difficulty. In this way, we can put in order the stages of his mission, which have been listed by many commentators—such as Fahreddin Razi—correctly but in no particular order.[5] Such an order may shed light on certain principles that could be beneficial in our day. In the verses regarding Abraham's invitation and teaching, the audience is sometimes only his father, sometimes only his people, and sometimes both his father and his people. There is also a speech directed only to Nimrod. In these verses sometimes only Abraham is mentioned, and sometimes Abraham and the people with him are both mentioned (showing that he now had followers).

Based on these different audiences and some other evidence, it is possible to detail some of the stages in his prophetic mission and even to put these stages in a tentative chronological order. Although there might be a slight possibility of error, some degree of extrapolation can reasonably be made from the information in the verses. As a matter of fact, Fahreddin Razi and other leading commentators always strive to bring many and varied approaches and analytical tools to such verses.

One logical deduction is to assume that when Abraham addressed only his father, it was the beginning of his mission, because as a principle Prophets begin by inviting their families first. This is evident in the life of Prophet Muhammad and is established in some verses of the Qur'an.[4]

If we are correct in this assumption about Prophet Abraham, then his exhortation directed only to his people must have come later. We can take the speech directed to both his father and his nation—as narrated by God in the Qur'an—as a summary of his communication with them up to that time, both individually and collectively. If it is instead a single speech, then it is also possible to see it as one of Abraham's last addresses to his people when his father was with them. This seems logical because the Qur'an is clear on the point that Abraham's father Azar did not turn from his unbelief and continued to reject the message. Indeed, some of the verses mention Abraham's exhortation on different occasions to his nation and/or his father- and their rejection of the invitation- in order to indicate that his father opposed him along with his people until the end. These episodes also show Abraham's solitariness in his struggle to submit to the Lord of the worlds, with none but the same (God) to trust and rely on, even among his own family—especially at the beginning of his mission, up until he was thrown into the fire.

Thus, it is possible to analyze Abraham's widening audience by distinguishing three phases:

a. His personal logical quest to understand the essentials of faith,

b. In the person of his father, his invitation to his family,

c. His public invitation to the society.

Having a Firm Faith

Abraham's journey to faith in God is narrated as a separate story in the Qur'an. Based on this narration, it can be discerned that he made a mental and spiritual journeying to have certainty of faith.

We would like to note here that in the verses which narrate this story, Abraham initially looks at "a star," "the moon," and "the sun" and declares for each one of them in turn, "This is my Lord!" In the end he states, "Whatever sets cannot be my Lord!" This requires a closer look beyond the surface. This story, rather than a literal account, is an indication of his process of leading his people to true faith. Otherwise it would be necessary to accept that Abraham held false beliefs, for however short a time. No reliable commentator of the Qur'an would accept this approach. As will become evident when we go into the techniques he chose in struggling with the polytheists, it is not possible to derive such a meaning from the above mentioned verses; taken together, it seems evident that these verses instead introduce us to Abraham's method of struggle in overcoming the polytheists.

The above mentioned verses also support another point: Logical reasoning must have had a prime role in Abraham's reaching perfect certainty of faith. This story points out the aspect of individual conscience which is at the heart of the Abrahamic faith, and will make it flourish with divine guidance to reach a splendid perfection like the Tuba-tree of Heaven. It is to reveal this hidden kernel, which is like the seed of the religion of Abraham, that God Almighty presents Abraham's story on the transient nature of the star, the moon and the sun, which he utilized to overcome the argument for polytheism by way of narrating his personal experience.

It seems that the prevalent faith of the society Abraham lived in involved the worship of stars. This is a stronger possibility. The stars, the moon, and the sun were worshipped for their light-giving properties by his entire society- from the highest rulers to the lowliest shepherds, from the scholars to the most unlearned- including those closest to him, his parents. By pretending to take them as lords one by one, he tried to make them understand that none of these finite things—*those that set*—could be their real Lord. He was rewarded for his searching and contemplation with divine guidance; he was honored with the display of the world of angels of this world and the heavens; he reached perfection and the pinnacle of faith.

Abraham's exploration and rational attainment of faith is not only related to belief in God. Once he reached the pinnacle of faith in the oneness of God, he brought to God his questions regarding the resurrection of the dead and thus was led to complete his faith in the Hereafter.

We can conclude by looking at the way he approached these two essential aspects of faith that Abraham's perfect understanding and belief in other aspects of faith came after similar rational consideration. In fact, Prophet Muhammad, who followed the path of Abraham, also had challenges to struggle with at the beginning of his Prophethood, when he first received revelation; before beginning his mission of inviting his people to the right path, before reaching perfection and the pinnacle of faith, he went through a period called "interruption of revelation," which scholars agree lasted three years).

Only after reaching this level of certainty of faith did Abraham start teaching his people, and in realizing this mission he chose to begin by showing the transient nature of things.

He started inviting first his family, especially his father. His invitation efforts with his family and nation must have been according to a certain plan and a process lasting months or years. It is only natural that there would be changes and developments throughout this process in response to the changing psychological conditions and the reactions of his interlocutors.

Invitation at the Family Level

We should note regarding Abraham's invitation of his family that the information given in the Qur'an is about his invitation of his father. The other members of the family are not discussed. However, judging from his speeches to his father we can assume that—after reaching certain faith at the individual level—he invited his family as a second step. In fact this step is quite evident in the case of Prophet Muhammad. This stage in his life began with the revelation of the verse: *And warn your nearest kinsfolk* (Shuara 26:214). There are many verses on Abraham's exhortation to his father and his disputes with him. The best example of such verses is found in chapter Maryam (19:41-49).

Before going into the details of this back-and-forth between Abraham and his father, it is important to bring up the following point: in the Qur'an Prophet Luqman is held up as the standard for children's upbringing and education.[5] The same principle is further shown in Prophet Noah's efforts for his son, although in the end these efforts were in vain. For in this effort, despite the son's insistence on rejection, there was always the prayer and the hope until the end of his life that "he might be saved."[6] Indeed, as stated in *hadith,* even if a person continually commits sins that will draw him very close to Hellfire, it is not impossible that he could attain salvation at the last minute and be admitted to Heaven.[7]

Another dimension of Qur'anic raising of children is shown by Prophet Jacob. He exemplifies close attention to his children, compassionate love for youth, patience and reliance on God in all difficulties. These examples are all instances showing the guidance and care of fathers for their children.

A son guiding his father is mentioned only in Abraham's case. His mission to teach his father formed one of his more original characteristics.

Like other topics in the Qur'an, this theme of "teaching (one's) father" in the life of the Prophet Abraham is not mentioned only once as if it had been an isolated incident; instead, it must be perceived as an example of "enlightening those above us," one of several types of teaching duties of the Messengers, the effects of which will last until the end of time. Prophet Abraham is given as the example to follow in the way he performed the various aspects of his duty to guide others.

Broadening this principle beyond the immediate relationship of children to parents, we find it has implications for any relationship with someone "above" oneself. This can be understood to be relevant for any teacher in trying to reach those with whom they have a close but respectful relationship, such as parents, aunts and uncles, grandparents, and even instructors, bosses etc. Further, Islamic scholars emphasize that those who have earned higher degrees of education, authority and station must also be shown deference, irrespective of age or blood ties.

After a close analysis of the verses dealing with this aspect of Prophet Abraham's life, and pointing out some important conclusions supported by the verses, we will continue with further examples:

> And make mention of Abraham in the Book. He was surely a sincere man of truth, a Prophet. When he said to his father: "O my father! Why do you worship that which neither hears nor sees, nor can in anything avail you? O my father! There has indeed come to me of knowledge (of truth) such as has never come to you, so follow me, and I will guide you to an even, straight path. O my father! Do not worship Satan (by obeying his whispering to you to worship idols)! Satan is ever rebellious against the All-Merciful. O my father! I am fearful lest a punishment from the All-Merciful befall you, and then you will become a close friend of Satan (and an instrument in his hand)." (Maryam 19: 41-45).

A careful look shows the respectful and gentle nature of this exhortation. He explains the truth without using sarcastic, accusatory, hurtful or harsh language. Putting his father's feelings first, he repeats several times affectionately, "my father," showing his love and respect.

His father does not accept this invitation, instead giving a hostile response:

> His father said: "Have you turned away from my deities, O Abraham? If you do not desist, I will surely cause you to be stoned! Now get away from me for a long while!" (Maryam 19:46)

There is a strong possibility that, like the dispute in the public assembly described in the Qur'an, the episode related here is in reality a summary of several debates, since it is unlikely that Azar would have responded so harshly to the first invitation of his son Abraham. A similar progression can be seen in the mission of Prophet Muhammad. All the details of his prophethood show that the threats and reactions he received from those who opposed him became more determined and harsh with time.

Thus, we can be certain that before these harsh reproofs, they had tried many ways to silence Prophet Abraham's warnings, requests, and criticism of idols: attractive promises of women, money and power; threats; even accusations that he was possessed or mentally disordered. For all of these were suffered by Prophet Muhammad too. This is the natural gradual.

With these points in mind, we can see each of the following in the message Abraham presented to his father:

1. That the attributes of the true God include seeing, knowing, and granting blessings to His creatures,
2. That he was divinely inspired, or more specifically, was a prophet (messenger of God),
3. That worshipping Satan is folly and specifically, that Satan is an enemy of the Most Merciful,
4. That following the wrong path results in divine punishment,

After establishing these four principles and their corresponding phases of teaching, the Qur'an turns to the father's attitude and stance.

Azar's response went through the following stages, in correspondence with the stages of Abraham's message as outlined above:

1. Upon hearing the message he opposed it right away, and warned Abraham,

2. He did not accept the prophethood of Abraham,

3. He perceived that his son's mission was to struggle against idolatry, and tried to get him to give this up. To imagine what he may have done to try to accomplish this, it is enough to consider the uncle of Prophet Muhammad, Abu Talib, who died upon his ancestors' belief, and even more, Abu Lahab, who intervened after Abu Talib's death. These two swayed between protective feelings one normally has for relatives and maliciousness arising from their unbelief. In fact there is a striking parallel between the final opposing stance struck by Abu Lahab and that of Azar.

4. The heavy punishments that were threatened, summarized by the word "stoning";

5. Being expelled out of his father's house. His entire community was antagonistic toward him, and it was no small punishment to be ejected from his family's home into a society where he could find no acceptance or help from anywhere. This is reminiscent of the time when, under pressure from Qurayshi tribesmen who wanted to attack Prophet Muhammad, his uncle Abu Talib said, "My nephew, do not lay on me a burden too heavy for me to carry"; the reply was, "Uncle, if you were even to put the sun in my right hand, and the moon in the left, I will never give up preaching my cause," and his determination softened Abu Talib.

There could be no greater difficulty for Azar to inflict on Prophet Abraham than to throw him out of his house and leave his son without protection in that hostile environment, and yet that is what he did.

Prophet Abraham had to cease trying to convince his father of his message. But in telling his father so, he spoke gently, avoided cutting ties, and said that he continued to hope for his enlightenment:

> He said: "Peace be upon you! I will pray to my Lord to forgive you. Surely He has been ever gracious to me. (Maryam 19:47)

In the Qur'anic summary of this sharp disagreement, although at first it may appear that the conversation with his father continued uninterrupted, a closer look seems to show that a long interval must have passed:

> And I will withdraw from you (my father and my people), and from whatever you deify and invoke other than God. I pray to my Lord alone; I hope that I will not be unblessed in my prayer to my Lord. (Maryam 19:48)

Based on two pieces of evidence I argue this statement represented a break in communication:

1. The style is harsher compared to the previous statements,
2. In this verse the statement is no longer directed toward only one person (his father), but to his people. Where before the invitations and exhortations were directed toward his father, this one uses the plural "you": "But I shall withdraw from you all and from whatever you (all) invoke instead of God..."

Thus, the estrangement mentioned in this verse is not estrangement from his father, but has greater meaning: It signifies the emigrationthat occurred in Prophet Abraham's life after his people attempted to execute him by fire. In fact, the following verse clearly implies that this is the point at which he went into exile: *And after he had withdrawn from them and from all that they were worshipping instead of God, We bestowed upon him Isaac and Jacob...* (Maryam 19:49).

Therefore it is possible to say that Prophet Abraham, maintained a courteous demeanor with his father and even hopedfor his sake that he could attain to faith, until he broke with his people. As a matter of fact the verse I am about to mention seems to speak of the time of breaking with them. For here we see that as he speaks to his father, he also brings up his people. At this point he must have seen there was nolonger hope for his people or his father to change their minds. This being the case, he had no remaining choice but to speak up for truth straightforwardly: *And lo, thus spoke Abraham unto his father Azar: "Do you take idols for deities? Indeed, I see you and your people lost in obvious error"* (Anam 6:74).

This strong statement was meant to move them to see the serious need to change. It is clear that this was no minor matter, but an accusation of heresy. Fahreddin Razi also points out that the strength of this statement resulted from the length of the struggle to convince them up to this point; it was a last attempt after a long period of unsuccessful attempts.[8]

We must note that there is a similarity here between Prophet Abraham and Prophet Noah: continuing to hope and pray for those close to them until the very last moment, and continuing to do what was in their power to show them the right way. Just as Noah tried to convince his son to choose the right even in the last moments of the latter's life,[9] so also he was true to his wife until her dying breath. Although a Qur'anic verse gives her as a negative example, it still mentions her as "Noah's wife." This means that despite her unbelief and rebellion, he honored his wedding vows, instead of sending her away or divorcing her.[10] Prophet Muhammad also showed this kind of compassion for his uncle Abu Talib, and was moved to tears of sadness when his uncle died uttering, "I remain in the religion of my fathers."

Thus we can say that one of the principles Prophet Abraham passed on to all believers, through his actions in these matters, is to never give up hope in trying to awaken others from heedlessness, and continue to strive for their enlightenment until the very last, despite all that may have gone before.

Exhorting his people

It can be said that after Prophet Abraham was rejected by his father and even received a definite "no" from him, he turned to his people. Of course, this does not mean that he ceased his efforts with his father. Here another issue comes to mind: of the exhortations to his people recorded in the Qur'an, which was chronologically first?

The answer is not clear. However, the most likely candidate is in chapter 6, where Prophet Abraham seems to make logical conclusions about the stars and how they could not be his Sustainer; this could be a rhetorical tool he was using to explain to his people the oneness of God. The verse says:

> When the night overspread over him, he saw a star; and he exclaimed: "This is my Lord, (is it)?" But when it set (sank from sight), he said: "I love not the things that set." And when (on another night), he beheld the full moon rising in splendor, he said: "This is my Lord, (is it)!" But when it set, he said: "Unless my Lord guided me, I would surely be among the people gone astray." Then, when he beheld the sun rising in all its splendor, he said: "This is my Lord, (is it)? This one is the greatest of all!" But when it set, he said: "O my people! Surely I am free from your association of partners with God and from whatever you associate with Him as partners. I have turned my face (my whole being) with pure faith and submission to the One Who has originated the heavens and the earth each with particular features, and I am not one of those associating partners with God."
>
> His people set out to remonstrate with him. (Anam 6:76-80)

Although it is not certain, I identify this as Prophet Abraham's first address to his people based on the following clues:

1- Razi discusses various possibilities in considering the meaning of this verse. In his opinion, Prophet Abraham uttered these sentences as a rational proof against idol worship, hoping thereby to capture the attention of his people. His basic intention was to demonstrate that a mortal being, or "things that set" (such as the sun and moon), cannot be a worthy object of worship. Rather than contradict their beliefs directly, he began by justifying his own beliefs. He first said, "This (star) is my Lord (is it)!" but when it went down, he said, "I love not the things that set." Thus he rejected his first statement, giving the rational reasoning. In the same way he rejected and proved wrong the idea that the moon or sun could be the Sustainer, showing that no mortal being could sustain the universe.[11]

Thus, this exchange gives the impression of being one of the first times Abraham addressed his people with his divine message. His method was friendly and gentle, attempting to persuade and convince them.

Hamdi Yazir construes these verses to mean that on his spiritual journey to *tawhid*, or fully understanding God's oneness, Prophet Abraham followed an intellectual and rational path; "When he had yet to reach the spiritual peaks and before prophethood had been conferred upon him, he went through a rational searching process, and came to the conclusion that the universe was created." He also explains in another place that when Prophet Abraham said of the star, moon and sun in turn, "This is my Sustainer (?)" he was not expressing his true beliefs, but was employing this rhetorical tool to expose the logical fallacy in these statements and prove these beliefs false.

2- After this soliloquy which he delivered as though he were reasoning to himself—when the sun too set—Prophet Abraham began preaching to his audience and declared to them in no uncertain terms that mortal beings such as the sun, moon and stars, no matter how great or how helpful, could not be gods—nor could anything which had no power in itself and was subject to death.

As we know, Prophet Abraham's people worshipped the stars.[12] Prophet Abraham expertly and adeptly expounded with flawless logic the falsehood of ascribing divinity to anything beside God, and the truth of the existence of the One God, in a way that would arouse their curiosity and command their attention.

Here, one may wonder why didn't his people protest at the very beginning, when he said "I love not the things that set" instead of reacting to his statements after the sun set.

This question needs to be answered by taking his gradual approach into consideration. We may infer that at the beginning he tried not to give his message straightforwardly so that people did not keep away from him. They probably assumed that Abraham more or less held a similar belief to their own. He must have left his true message to the end deliberately and tried to teach about his religion through the process; the gradual process which later ended with his breaking the idols, being imprisoned, and finally thrown into the fire.

He survived the fire as a miracle but the unbelief of his people was unlikely to change. Having done all he could, he emigrated from the landof Nimrodin order to continue his mission in other places.

GRADUAL PROGRESSION OF CONTENT

After analyzing the progression in widening his audience it is also important to examine the stages and progression in the content of his message. I think it is appropriate to briefly deal with this subject. I say "briefly" because there is limited material on this subject related to the content of Prophet Abraham's teaching. The material at hand is more related to the gradual progression of his mission with regard to the widening of his audience. Yet this progression in content is significant and necessary if my main message is to be understood and accepted.

In fact this concept can be observed in detail in the prophetic mission of Prophet Muhammad. A close look at the gradualness of the former's mission makes it possible to deduce the significance of gradualness in Prophet Abraham's teachings. For instance, there was gradualness in the way Prophet Muhammad taught, from small institutions such as starting all good deeds by saying "In the name of Allah," to the essential acts of worship such as the five daily prayers, fasting, and almsgiving, and even in issues related with faith. Fahreddin Razi, considering Abraham's reference to celestial beings in turn (stars, the Moon and the Sun) from this perspective, states that "practicing gradualness by beginning from the lesser (star) and moving towards the greater (the Moon and lastly the Sun) was more effective as a rhetorical structure."[13]

Thus the mentioned text emphasizes the significant influence of gradualness and stages in the content of the preaching of Prophet Abraham.

In fact, if we analyze the issues[14] that Abraham focused in the initial stages of invitation towards Azar, we can observe a gradualness similar to that in the invitation of Prophet Muhammad. It is possible to mention five stages in his approach to his father that come one after another, and together form a complete whole:

1. To make God known (the One to be worshipped),
2. To make himself known as a prophet,
3. To make Satan known,
4. To warn of the life of the world to come,
5. To separate himself.

1- The following verse refers to the stage of making God known: *O my father! Why do you worship something that neither hears nor sees and can be of no avail whatever to you?* (Maryam 19:42)

At this stage Prophet Abraham refers to the basic characteristics of one that deserves to be worshipped:

– Should be all hearing,
– Should be all seeing,
– Should be powerful to do good or harm.

He is pointing out that only something that has all these features can be worthy of worship. According to the Qur'an, even the rejecters of faith agreed on the existence of the Creator of the heavens and the earth (Allah was their name for Him).[15] Therefore, Abraham does not bring evidence for the existence of God to his father, who already believes in Allah (God). Instead he focuses on his practices in worship, which contradict faith. This is the beginning of his struggle with the universal human tendency to attach divinity to things "fashioned by their own hands" and overlook their true Creator and His commands as a result of emotional preferences and this psychological Achilles heel.

Conscious of this human weakness, Prophet Abraham began by attempting to attract attention to the idea that hand-made things cannot be worthy of worship. Looking from this perspective at the issues that he raised in his first invitation of his father, we can add another point: Prophet Abraham reasoned thus with his father: "Oh my father! One that can see, hear and do good or harm is superior to one which cannot do any of these. Therefore human beings, since they can see, hear and do good or inflict harm, are superior to idols, which can do none of these. Then why would a human being worship something that is inferior and moreover hand-made?"

Certainly, someone who cannot object and respond to such a reasonable and unobjectionable idea that is in conformity with readily observed facts, will either submit and accept the truth or give inhumane and illogical reactions and responses. Prophet Abraham's father Azar's attitude exemplifies this. His responses were:

a.   To reject his son Abraham's invitation,
b.   To accuse his son Abraham of abandoning the faith of his ancestors and try to put him on the defensive,
c.   To threaten him with stoning if he would not give up and repent,
d.   When this threat did not work, to withdraw familial protection and to expel him.

The conversation between Abraham and his father presented in the verse as if it happened in one meeting or session must have happened over the course of months or even years. These ideas that seem to be expressed by Prophet Abraham and his father in one exchange must be the main points raised and discussed throughout a long process. It can be convincingly argued that these issues were covered in the same order as presented in the verse. In this case, Azar's expulsion of Abraham is the last scene in the sequence of Abraham's relations with his father. In fact, it seems reasonable Azar could have been declaring a decision that was reached together with his community.

Prophet Abraham must have discussed the idea that "the one worthy of worship must be hearing, seeing, and able to do good and harm" not only with his father, but also with the community. We know this from their encounter with him on the occasion when he had knocked down and broke the idols, and hung the ax on the biggest idol.

We would like to briefly point out an issue that we will discuss later in detail: The content of his invitation to his father and the content of the wider invitation to his people were the same. He must have presented same messages albeit at different times in the same order to both audiences. The necessity to divide it into two stages, familial invitation and national (or tribal) invitation, is firstly a result of the Qur'anic proof of such a division in Prophet Muhammad's prophethood, and secondly, supported by the existence of strong evidence in the verses about Prophet Abraham that makes it reasonable to extrapolate that it applied to his ministry as well.

2- *The Stage of Making Himself Known as a Prophet* is presented in the following verse: *O my father! To me has come knowledge which has not reached you: so follow me: I will guide you to a way that is even and straight* (Maryam 19:43).

Here Prophet Abraham is gently warning his father regarding the falsehood of the religion of his ancestors. For his father, to follow Abraham means abandoning the path that he has followed in imitation of his ancestors.

The only merit of this old religion is that it came from his ancestors. His father would in the end rely on this point in making his defense, or more correctly his offense, accusing and blaming Abraham for abandoning the faith of his ancestors.

At this point, the context tells us that it is easier to understand and accept the existence of God than it is to accept prophethood. For this reason Prophet Abraham first spoke of God and His basic attributes.

An Abrahamic message can be derived here: it is of the essence in religious education for beginners no matter their age to begin by helping them to understand God.

Indeed, Prophet Muhammad utilized the above mentioned Abrahamic method: the first task he gave to children who had just begun to speak was to memorize the following verse about God.

Say: "Praise be to Allah, who begets no son, and has no partner in (His) dominion: Nor (needs) He any to protect Him
from humiliation." (Isra 17:111)[16]

3- *The Stage of Introducing Satan*. This issue is handled following the issue of Prophethood. Firstly his rebellion against God is
mentioned, and then his punishment by fire as a result of this rebellion: "Oh Father! Do not worship Satan for, verily, Satan is a rebel
against the Most Gracious!"

Here it is mentioned that this rebellion is against the "Most
Gracious" (Ar-Rahim), that is, the One that provides all needs and
nourishes all created beings. Nourishment means all that benefits
us and sustains us, moment to moment all that allows our life to
continue. Since this shows that what he has rejected the Sustainer
and our being sustained is obvious and difficult to ignore, it points
out the weakness of Satan's reasoning and logical thinking. So the
message means, "Is it possible to follow such an unreasonable ingrate,
and those who follow him?"

A PRESUMPTION

I believe it is safe to make a presumption based on the evidence in
the Qur'an on this issue of gradualness. Did not Prophet Abraham,
while calling others to faith in the unity of God, take it as an important task to deal with some of the superstitions of his nation so that
they would listen to him? Yet timing was very important: superstitions were left for after the main points of his message. The Qur'anic
evidence that leads us to this presumption is the episode, before his
prophetic mission had begun, when, having decided to break their
idols (while they are at a festival), he looks at the stars and says (as
if divining from them), "I am sick." The key point is that when he
says this, people believe him and leave.[17] It seems logical that if pri-
or to this time he had criticized this superstition (divination by
looking at the stars), his people would not have believed him when
he looked at the stars, saying instead, "He does not believe in stars."
Yet they believe him, leave him, and go to their festival.

The Abrahamic message we can deduce here is this: It is not intelligent to dwell on details especially superstitions that are deeply rooted in the souls of individuals before essential issues, such as the unity of God, prophethood, life after death, worship, and justice, are sufficiently taken to heart and internalized. Such details should be left for later, and time should not be wasted on such issues in the beginning.

4- *The Stage of Warning.* If the efforts of the previous stages prove ineffective, the next step is to show the disastrous end to which the path of error leads. At this stage, Prophet Abraham reminds his father that he fears torment may find him and that Satan will befriend him in Hell: *"O my father! I dread lest a chastisement from the Most Gracious befall you, and then you will become aware of having been close unto Satan!"* (Maryam 19:45)

In these conversations, presumably in the beginning stage, Abraham always speaks to his father with words such as "Oh my father!" which arouse mercy and affection, indicating love and respect.

5- *The Stage of Separating Oneself.* At the end his father Azar was not convinced and threatened Abraham with stoning: *(His father) answered: "Do you dislike my gods, O Abraham? Indeed, if you desist not, I shall most certainly cause you to be stoned to death! Now be gone from me for good!"* (Maryam 19:46).

At this response, Prophet Abraham would abandon his invitation to his father, but not in the form of being completely hopeless and cutting off all ties. This was a separation with hope to gain him back: *He replied: "Peace be upon you! I shall ask my Sustainer to forgive you: for, behold, He has always been kind unto me. But I shall withdraw from you all and from whatever you invoke instead of God, and shall invoke my Sustainer alone: it may well be that my prayer for thee will not remain unanswered by my Sustainer"*(Maryam 19:47-48).

IS THERE A DIFFERENCE BETWEEN THE FAMILIAL AND SOCIETAL STAGES?

At this point it may be useful to state that in my opinion there is no serious difference, in terms of content and progression of topics, between Prophet Abraham's appeal to his father and his appeal to his nation. Moreover, I do not see much difference in the approach and methodology he used in dealing with the family and the society. The separation of his mission into these two stages is not a result of difference in content, but of technical needs: His approach with his family was restricted by his need for and reliance on familial protection in his wider invitation, and perhaps it also provided experience necessary for his societal invitation. It seems likely that all messengers "warmed up" in this way to the challenges of preaching their message widely. We know many details of this stage in the prophetic mission of Prophet Muhammad, for example.

The similarity of content and progression in both stages is apparent in one of the longest (comprising nearly two pages) Qur'anic passages on the Prophet Abraham's message to his people, verses 16-27 of chapter Ankabut. In this long set of verses the Prophet Abraham's prophetic mission is summarized: he commands to worship the One God; he teaches some attributes of God that were central to his basic message; his people react and attempt to execute him by fire; the Prophet Lot converts; subsequent exile; the bestowal of his children Isaac and Jacob; the granting of revelation and prophethood to his descendents.

If we assume that the events in Prophet Abraham's life took place in the same order as they are mentioned in this section of the Qur'an, we see that the invitation to worship God comes first. Due to the significance of this order, I will present them below as they are written in these verses, and assign a number to each separate issue that is brought up as part of his message. Aside from showing the order of introduction of topics, this highlights the fact that some issues are repeated. The second number will show the number of repetitions (so that 2/3 would represent the *third* mention or repetition of the *second* issue presented). Thus we will see how many times each issue is repeated. Certainly these are repeated due to their importance.

> And Abraham, too, (We sent as Messenger). He said to his people (in conveying this message): "Worship God alone and keep

from disobedience to Him in reverence for Him and piety. Doing so is the best for you, if you would know. (1) You worship only idols instead of God, (2) and thus you invent a mere falsehood. (3) Surely those (beings whom you deify and make statutes of, and idols) that you worship instead of God do not have power to provide for you; (4) so seek all your provision from God, (4/2) and worship Him (1/2) and be thankful to Him. (1/3) To Him you are being brought back. (5) If you deny Our Messenger, know that many communities before you denied (6). What rests with the Messenger is no more than to convey the Message fully and clearly. (6/2) Have they not considered how God originates creation in the first instance, (7) and then reproduces it? (5/2) This is indeed easy for God. (8) Say: "Go about on the earth and see how God originated creation. (7/2) Then God will bring forth the other (second) creation (in the form of the Hereafter). (5/3) Surely God has full power over everything. (1/4) (He will bring forth the Hereafter, where) He punishes whom He wills (9) and has mercy on whom He wills. (1/5) To Him you are being returned. (5/4) You cannot frustrate Him (1/6) in the earth or in the heaven. And you have none to protect you, and none to help you, except God. (1/7) Those who disbelieve in the signs of God (in the universe and in themselves) and His Revelations, and in the meeting with Him (in the Hereafter), they have no hope and expectation of a share in My Mercy. (2/2) (God has forbidden them Paradise.) And for them there is a painful punishment. (2/3) But the response of his (Abraham's) people was only to say: "Kill him, or burn him," (10) but God saved him from the fire (11). Surely in this are signs (important lessons) for people who will believe and who will deepen in faith. He (Abraham) said to them: "You have taken to yourselves idols to worship instead of God, for no other reason than to have a bond of love and attachment between you only in the life of this world. (12) But then, on the Day of Resurrection you will deny one another (disowning any relation between you), and curse one another. Your final refuge will be the Fire, (9/2) and you will have no helpers. (1/8) Lot believed in him, and he (Abraham) said: "I am emigrating to my Lord (leaving my land and people for a place where I can practice my Religion). Surely, He is the All-Glorious with irresistible might, the All-Wise. (1/9) We bestowed upon him (a son) Isaac and (a grandson) Jacob, and caused Prophethood and the revelation of the Book to continue among his off-spring, and We granted him his reward in this world also; and he surely is among the righteous in the Hereafter. (Maryam 29:16-27)

There are a few notable points in this Qur'anic summary of Prophet Abraham's life:

1. The episodes in which Prophet Abraham goes through his intellectual analysis of issues of faith are not mentioned in this section: proving the unity of God, rejecting star worship, breaking the idols, etc. Perhaps these issues are omitted here because they are detailed at length in other sections.

2. He continued to struggle against idol worship among his people after the incident of being thrown into the fire.

3. He began to collect followers after the fire incident. The Qur'an explicitly states that Lot believed at this point. Non-Qur'anic sources mention that Sarah joined the believers before his exile. However the word "followers" in the verse *Indeed, you have had a good example in Abraham and those who followed him, ...* (Mumtahana 60:4) points to the existence of at least three followers. Otherwise, the word "followers" here could have referred to the community of believers that increased in number after Prophet Abraham moved to Palestine, but that would not be in conformity with the verse above. Consequently, upon this Qur'anic indication, we can accept that there were believers other than Lot and Sarah after the fire incident and before immigration. The degree of harshness in the response of the believers, quoted in the continuation of the above-mentioned verse, confirms this assumption. They tell the idolators—after the latter had tried to execute Abraham—that "We are quit of you and whatever you worship besides God. We have rejected you (in your polytheism), and there has arisen between us and you enmity and hate forever until you believe in God alone."

This expression, as we saw before, indicates that Prophet Abraham was completely cut off from his people and was close to exile. Besides, as mentioned above, in the Qur'anic summary of the life of Prophet Abraham this separation and exile from his people is mentioned after the fire incident.[18]

THE THREE ESSENTIAL DYNAMICS OF THE ABRAHAMIC STRUGGLE

When we closely analyze the verses regarding the struggles of Abraham, we come across three essential principles which give spirit to the continuation and success of the struggle and are a kind of spiritual basis. All these three principles are imbedded in his pure and absolute belief in unity and his moral virtues:

- expecting nothing in return
- openness and courage
- careful planning

a) *Expecting nothing in return*: This refers to the fact that he did everything only to please God. His strong faith in God led him to meticulously practice all orders of God. Not only rejection of his message, but even threats to kill him and burn him did not prevent him from scrupulously fulfilling his mission. His selflessness is the result primarily of his pure and exalted level of *tawhid* (faith and understanding of the oneness of God), and of his other moral virtues.

b) *Open attitude*: A significant issue that attracts our attention in the verses related to Prophet Abraham's struggle is the fact that he conducted his struggle openly. That is, he very openly expressed his ideas to his father, to his people and to the authorities. He declared and broadcasted that their way was mistaken without any fear or worries. He expressed the truth as it is without falling into discouraging thoughts such as, "I am alone, I am weak; my opponents are many and physically powerful enough to easily snuff out my life; they have treasuries, armies, every kind of power..." Some of his acts which may seem at first glance to contradict this openness were in fact strategic first steps on the way to his ultimate goals. This point has been dealt with earlier in this text, with examples.

c. *Careful planning as a strategy*: Careful planning was indeed one of Abraham's defining characteristics. Too many who act openly and courageously generally lack planning. They do most things hastily and in an unorganized, un-thought-out way. The success of such an endeavor is usually very short lived even if it might bring bright moments of achievement. World literature has symbolized such brash, unthinking (unplanning) courage in "Don Quixote."

In Prophet Abraham's struggle we observe a preplanned program. He took the first steps after calculating his later steps, words and actions, and thus he was able to nimbly spar with his rejecting audience. We observe this careful planning clearly in the beginning of his prophethood when he started preaching, as well as in one of his most well known acts, breaking down the idols.

In the first instance, in order to point out how fallacious it is to worship celestial bodies, he openly stated "This is my Lord" for the stars, the moon, and the sun in turn so that none of his opponents objected. He kept his real argument to the end. When the sun, the biggest and the brightest of all their gods, went down and set like the others, he turned to his people and revealed that his real intention in pretending to be looking for a god in the skies was to reject idol-worship and star-worship. It was only then—after they had listened to his logical reasons for his stance—that he let them know he was against their practices, and only then that they were able to bring up objections. The more obvious and evident example of this methodology is the breaking down of the idols.

Although his dispute with the idol-worshippers seems to take place in a single meeting, in fact this is a Qur'anic summary of Abraham's main arguments and the continuous disputes that took place throughout long years of struggle. In other words, this is a summary of the most significant incidents and the major ideas that Abraham professed until his exile (emigration).

All invitations and declarations of Abraham were in vain, as the people on the whole were not aware of the seriousness of the matter. They mocked his invitations and took him for a joke. In order to awaken them, to make them earnestly think about the issue at hand, it was necessary to do something drastic and public. Prophet Abraham planned to crash their idols in order to make them realize that these idols cannot even protect themselves. However, the plan and timing had to be such that it should:

1. not be sensed beforehand.
2. first make them think.
3. make them argue amongst themselves,
4. make them feel, and even admit the wrongness of their way,
5. push them to reveal their true and final position.

Qur'anic commentaries mention that it was public festivalday; this is consistent with the verse. In this case Abraham did not participate in the festival that everyone else was attending. Looking at the stars, he said, "I am sick," and this legitimized his absence so that he would not cause any suspicion. Their practice of divination made them assume his statement was connected to his glance at the stars. In this way, Abraham utilized the traditions of the people in his plan, which allowed him to avoid the plan being discovered. Since Abraham looked at the stars and said "I am sick," the incident must have taken place at night. This star-worshipping people might have held their festival at night, so that the stars would be most visible. If it had been daytime, presumably the worship house would have been occupied by a guard, custodian, visitor, worshipper, etc. He wouldn't have been free to knock down the idols; he could have been faced with a surprise or even caught red-handed. Certainly he was not avoiding these because he feared the consequences, but rather for the success of the plan and its desired result. He knew that he would be caught eventually. But with this plan he aimed at having people think about the error of their ways and hoped to have them admit to themselves, "We are wrong!"

To throw Abraham's plan into high relief, I will mention the interpretation of Tabari on this issue. According to him, when Abraham was asked "Did you break the idols?" he responded in a way calculated to first surprise the idol worshippers, then lead them to contemplation, and lastly to make them contradict themselves. He said in effect, "Rather, (some doer) must have done it—this is the biggest of them."

This explanation sounded reasonable to his audience. Giving up the argument that "Abraham broke them," they started discussing the issue. At some point at least some of them said "Behold, it is you who are wrong," which Asad explains in his footnote as "you are doing wrong to Abraham by rashly suspecting him"; or, according to Tabari, "We have done an injustice to Abraham—it must have happened the way he told us." The debate went on between them. In the end they relapsed into their former way of believing and said to Abraham: "You know very well that these idols cannot speak."[19]

That is exactly what Abraham was trying to get them say. They were forced to admit the error of their beliefs to themselves. He can now drive home the point:

> "Then, do you then worship, instead of God, that which can- not benefit you in any way, nor harm you? Shame onyou and on all that you worship instead of God! Will you not reason and understand?" (Anbiya 21:65-66)

Abraham expressed this truth after putting them in an indefen- sible position. In order to bring them to such a situation he imple- mented a well thought-out plan which went through several phases.

In sum, I argue that if it had not been for Abraham's minute- ly detailed long-term plan, laid in conformity with the psychologi- cal state of his audience, his selflessness could have been more like naiveté or gullibility, and his courage would have resembled that of Don Quixote.

Humanity, through the faith of Abraham, can reach the peace- ful state of being the nation of Abraham once again. In the Prophet Muhammad's words, there shall be global peace on Earth[20] through brotherhood and sisterhood in the Prophet Abraham to such a degree that lions and camels, tigers and cattle will graze together without harming each other, and a child will play with a snake, even putting her hand into its mouth, without being hurt.[21] It is the responsibil- ity of people who love peace to bring to life this message.

NOTES

INTRODUCTION

[1] However, Prophet Muhammad being mentioned by name only 4 times in the Qur'an does not serve as a criterion for comparison among the other prophets. This is because the Qur'an was addressed to him, and therefore, every command was also addressed to him. In addition to these command forms, such as "Say!" it is possible to add the phrase "O Muhammad," meaning "O Muhammad, teach the people the following truth!" Thus when taking into account these indirect references along with occurrences of his name, it is likely that the references to Prophet Muhammad would greatly outnumber the total number of references to all other Prophets.

[2] Razi, *Tafsir*, 4,33.

[3] Rodinson, *Mahomet*, p. 219.

[4] Buhl, *L'Encyclopedie de l'Islam*, 1 ere edt. 3,695.

[5] *See* Hajj 22:78.

[6] As Wilhelm Schmidt argued, accepting that Abraham was the first person to preach the Islamic doctrine of tawhid (the Oneness of God) invalidates the theory that religion evolved from animism to fetishism, from polytheism to monotheism, Judaism, Christianity, and finally to Islam.

[7] *Musnad*, 6, 116, 233; 5,266.

PART ONE
THE LIFE OF PROPHET ABRAHAM

[1] *See* Mu'jam al-Buldan 5,402; Elmalili, *Tafsir* 3,1965; Tumer, "Azer", DIA 4,316-317; Ibn Sa'd, *Tabaqat* 1,46; Tabari, *History* 1,233, 256, 310, Ibn al-Asir al-Kamil 1, 94.

[2] According to Tabari (one of the four main hadith collections), the city was named after its founder Haran, who was Prophet Abraham's brother and the father of Prophet Lot.

[3] Tabari, *History* 1,233 ; Ibn Sa'd, *Tabaqat* 1,46.

[4] Wensinck, *Islam Ansiklopedisi* (Encyclopedia of Islam), "Ibrahim," M.E.B. (Ministry of Education Publication), Istanbul: 1950, Vol. 5, p. 878.

[5] Regarding the numbers found in Islamic sources for the age of the creation and the world, Ibn Hazin writes, "When it comes to the dispute on the matter of time, Jews say the world is some 4,000 years old. Christians estimate it to be 5,000 years old. For Muslims, no exact known date exists. Those who say it is

7,000, or more or less, are mistaken. There has never been any authentic tradition from Prophet Muhammad on this issue. On the contrary, there is a hadith acknowledging the dispute. Thus we can say confidently, "only God knows the age of the Earth." Indeed, in one verse Almighty God says, "I did not make them witness the creation of the Heavens and the Earth, nor of the creation of their own selves. . . " (Kahf 18:51) (Ibn Hazin, *al-Fasl Fi'l-Milal* 2,105-106. Ibn Kathir also states that there is no authentic tradition regarding the time when the Last Day will occur. (*an-Nihaya fi'l-Fitan*, 1,15).

[6]   Ibn Sa'd, *Tabaqat*, 1, 53.

[7]   The verse Al Imran 3:67 confirms that Abraham never worshipped idols: *He (Abraham) was never of those who associate partners with God.*

[8]   Ibn al-Athir, *al-Kamil* 1, 94-95.

[9]   Elmalili Hamdi Yazir, *Tafsir* 3, 1962-1963.

[10] This place was called Sab, meaning seven, because there were seven wells. (*Mu'jam al-Buldan* 3,185)

[11] Ibn al Athir, *al-Kamil*, 1,102, Tabari, 1,24

[12] Ibid

[13] Ibn Sa'd 1, 46-47. *See* Tabari, *History* 1,310-311.

[14] Ibid. 1,48

[15] Ibid

[16] Tabari, 1,311.

[17] Ibn al-Athir, *al-Kamil*, 1, 94.

[18] Ibid. l, 95.

[19] Tabari 1, 310.

[20] Ibid 1, 311.

[21] Ibid.1, 311.

[22] Ibid. 1, 249.

[23] Ibn al-Athir, ibid., 1, 111.

[24] Sarah's dying of grief gives a picture that is completely opposed to that related in the main body of narrations, in which Ishmael's mother Hagar, like her son and husband, is totally accepting of God's will. Tabari, 1, 249, Ibn al-Athir 1, 123. In a narration of Ibn al-Athir, Sarah was 70 at this time. However, in the Qur'an her reaction to the annunciation of the birth of Prophet Isaac, "Being withered up, how can I conceive?" increases the likelihood that she was 90. I would like to draw attention to a conflict in this version. It says that Sarah, who was pregnant with Isaac at the age of 90, died of grief at 127 on hearing that he would be sacrificed. This would make Isaac 36, but the same tradition says he was 16. In the other version where Ishmael was to be sacrificed, Hagar accepted this news with great submission to God. In addition, based on authentic hadith, Hagar died not at the time of the near-sacrifice, but after the marriage of Ishmael.

25 Ibn Sa'd, 1,48.

26 Razi, *Tafsir*, 7,23.

27 Razi, *Tafsir*, 22,187.

28 Tabari, 1, 312.

PART TWO
THE VIRTUES OF THE PROPHET ABRAHAM

1 Bukhari, *Anbiya* ll, Tafsir, Baqara 46; Muslim, *Iman*, 238.

2 Ibn Hajar, *Fath al-Bari* 7,223.

3 Ibid. 7,224.

4 Baqara 2:135; Al Imran 3:67, 95; Anam 6:161; Nahl 16: l6, 123.

5 An'am 6:79.

6. *See* Razi, ibid. 18, 224.

7 Said Nursi, *The Flashes Collection*, 11th Flash, Sozler Publications. Istanbul: 2003.

8 Hakim, *al-Mustadrak,* 2,291.

9 Ibn Maja, *Zuhd* 8, (4135,4136.); Tirmidhi, *Zuhd* 42.

10 Ibn Maja, *Fitan* 16(3989.h); Tirmidhi, *Nuzur* 9; *Musnad* 4,126.

11 Ahmad Ibn Hanbal, *Musnad* 2,60.

12 Tirmidhi, *Siyar,* 46.

13 Abu Dawud, *Tib,* 17; Ibn Maja, *Tib* 39

14 Razi, *Tafsir,* 20,135.

15 Mumtahana 60:4.

16 Razi, ibid. 4, 71-72.

17 *See* Bukhari, *Ahkam,* 43; Muslim, *Imara,* 41,42; Nasai, *Buyu* 44, *Bay'at* 1, 2, 4, 5.

18 Bukhari, *Tafsir*, Isra 5, (6,106).

19 Bukhari, *Anbiya*, 8; Muslim, *Fadail*, 154.

20 Bukhari, *Tafsir*, Isra 5, (6,106).

21 Ibn Hajar, *Fath al-Bari,* 7,201.

22 Elmalılı, Tafsir 6, 4061.

23 *Al-Nihaya,* l, 451.

24 Ibn al-Hajar, *al-Matalib al-Aliya*, 3, 30.

25 Bukhari, *Iman*, 29; *Musnad*, 1,236.

26 *Musnad*, 4, 338, 5, 32.

27 Bukhari, *Manaqib* 27; Adab, 80; Muslim, *Fadail*, 77, 78; Abu Dawud, *Adab*, 4; Muwatta, *Husn al-Khulq* 2; *Musnad* 6,85.

28 Bukhari, Iman, 29; Nasai, Iman 28; *Musnad* 4,422, 5, 350, 351.

29 Tabari 1, 286; *Musnad* 3, 439.

30 Tabari 1, 286-287.

31 Suyuti, *al-Fath al-Kabir*, Beirut:1351, 2,200.

32   Nursi, *The Letters*.

33   Baqara 2:125.

34   Ibn Kathir, *Tafsir* 6,461.

35   *See* Hamdi Yazir, *Tafsir* 7,4608.

36   Tabari l,285.

37   Razi, ibid. 4, 37-39.

38   Muslim, *Tahara*, 56; Ibn Maja, *Tahara*, 8, (253).

39   Baydawi, *Tafsir*, l, 35; Tabari 1, 279.

40   Tabari, ibid. 1, 279

41   Razi, ibid. 4, 38.

42   Tabari, 1, 281.

43   Ibn Kathir, *Tafsir* 6, 69; Ibn Sa'd, *Tabaqat* 1, 47.

44   Dhariyat 51:25-30; Hud, 11: 69.

45   Sad 38:45-47.

46   Sabuni, *Saffat al-Tafasir* 3,61.

47   Baydawi, *Tafsir* 2,158.

48   Ibn Hajar, *Fath al-Bari*, 7,197.

49   *See* Hamdi Yazir, 6,4060; Razi, *Tafsir* 26,146.

50   *See* Ibn Hajar, *Fath al-Bari*, 7,196; Elmalili, *Tafsir*, 1, 491.

51   Suyuti, *Durr al-Mansur*, 3, 24.

52   The issue of imprisonment was mentioned before.

53   Anbiya 21:68.

54   Maryam 19:46.

55   Waqidi, ibid. 1, 109.

56   Ibrahim 14:36.

57   Muslim, *Birr* 87.

58   Halabi, Ali Ibn Burhaneddin, *Sirat al-Halabiya*, Beirut, 1, 357; 2, 256.

59   Anbiya 21:107.

60   Halabi, ibid. 1, 357. Despite the fact that the verse honoring Prophet Muhammad with the titles *Rauf* and *Rahim* were revealed later in his life, the angel said this sometime in the early years of Prophethood; as Zurkani explains, "the angel must have been given prior knowledge of these characteristics," and thus there is no contradiction in the angel's saying it before the verses were revealed (*Sharh al-Mawahib al-Ladunniyya* 1,298).

61   People of the Book (Christians and Jews) living under Muslim rule.

62   Suyuti, *Fath al-Kabir* 3,144.

63   Bukhari, *Mazalim* 23; Muslim, *Salam* 153.

64   Anbiya 21:107.

65   Qur'an 9: 114.

66   Tirmidhi, *Zuhd* 45.

67   *Fayz al-Qadr* 3,71.

68   Suyuti, *al-Jami al-Saghir*.

69   *Musnad* 3,153; 2,367, also see Bukhari, 63.

70   Turan, Osman, *Turk Cihan Hakimiyeti Mefkuresi Tarihi,* Istanbul, 1969, 2,162.

71   Nahl 16:125.

72   Translator's note: *din* denotes both religion/faith and "moral law."

73   Baqara 2:256

74   When the Banu-Nadir Jews were exiled from Madina, conflict arose when they refused to turn over the Medinan children they had raised as Jews. This verse was revealed at the time of this conflict. (Ibn Kathir, *Tafsir* 1,551).

75   Nisa 4:97.

76   Ibn Hisham, *Sira*, 2,285.

77   Ibid. 1-2,419; Zurkani, Sharh al-Mawakib al-Ladunniya, 1,296-297.

78   The importance of emigration (*hijra*) in Islam is explained from various perspectives in my book *Teblig, Terbiye ve Siyasi Taktik Acilarindan Hicret* (Emigration for Conveying the Message, Moral Education, and Political Strategy), Yeni Asya, Istanbul: 1981. See also *Kutub-i Sitte Tercume ve Serhi* (Translation and Commentary of the Six Books of Hadith), Vol 16, pp.212-237.

79   Tabari, ibid.1, 244.

80   Tabari 1, 292-293.

81   Ibid. 1,244.

82   Commentators also note an ambiguity in one of the words: "*There is none besides us in this (world / land) who believes.*" Ibn Hajar suggests interpreting the word in question as "this land" and not "this world" since we know that Prophet Lot believed at this time. This remains an open question. (*Fath al-Bari* 7, 203)

83   Musnad, 1, 90.

84   Ibn al-Athir, *al-Nihaya* 1,68.

85   Razi, *Tafsir*, 20, 134-135.

86   Nursi, the Damascus Sermon.

87   Ibn Kathir, *Tafsir* 3,10, *See* An'am 6:12.

88   His prayers and entreaties to God for his unbelieving father, whom he worked so hard to convince without success, were so frequent and excessive that the Almighty gave him a warning (which will be touched on later).

    The example he provided to those of his line who came after him must be mentioned here. For, as I will demonstrate with verses some pages later in the section "Distinguished Descendants," his Lord accepted his prayers and requests for a line of descendants, due to his successes in passing the tests and carrying out the tasks he was given.

89   Nursi, S., *The Rays*, Sixth Ray, Sözler Publications, Istanbul: 2002, p. 120-121.

[90] Mawdudi shares the view that the Prophet Abraham was given the leadership of the humanity after succeeding in all the tests and trials (Tafhim 1,121). Sayyid Qutb also agrees on this point. (Fi zilal 1,237).

[91] Razi, ibid. 4,38.

[92] Nursi, *The Letters*, Seeds of truth.

[93] Nursi, *The Words*, The Twenty-ninth Word, Second Argument.

[94] Commentaries such as Muhammad Hamidullah. (Islamic Prophets 1, 136).

[95] Bukhari, *Badu'l Khalq*, 6, Anbiya, 22, 43; Muslim, *Faith* 264.

[96] Ibn Abi Jamra, *Bahjat al-Nufus*, 2, Beirut: 1972, 3, 195.

[97] Ibn Hajar, *Fath al-Bari*, 6,196.

[98] Razi, ibid. 11,56.

[99] ibid.

[100] Najm 53:36-37, Ala 87:18-19.

[101] Abu Dawud, *Fitan* 1, 4242.

[102] Sayyid Qutb, *Fi zilal al-Qur'an* 1,239.

[103] Muslim, *Fadail*, 23.

[104] Muslim, *Masajid*, 23.

[105] Al Imran 3:173.

[106] Bukhari, *Tafsir*, Al Imran 13.

[107] Muwatta, *Sifat al-Nabi* 4; Ibn Sa'd, ibid. 1,47; *See* Tabari 1,311.

[108] Ibid.

[109] Ibid.

[110] *See* Abu Dawud, *Tarajjul*, 17; Tirmidhi, *Fadail al-Jihad* 9; Musnad, 2, 312, 3,179, 307, 310.

[111] At the time of Prophet Abraham people were wearing robes; he was the first to wear the trousers under the robe in order not to expose his body, an indication of his piety. *See* Ibn Hajar, *Fath al-Bari*, 14,173.

[112] Bukhari, Anbiya 8,48, Tafsir, *Maidah* 4, 21; Muslim, *Jannah*, 58.

[113] Ibn Hajar, *Fath al-Bari* 14,174.

[114] Ibn Sa'd 1, 50.

[115] Muslim, *Tahara*, 56; Abu Dawud, *Tahara*, 29; Tirmidhi, *Adab* 14; Nasai, *Tahara*, 1; Ibn Maja, *Tahara*, 8, (293).

PART THREE
THE SERVICE OF PROPHET ABRAHAM

[1] Ibid, 3, 287-288.

[2] Bukhari, *Anbiya* 9, (4, 174).

[3] Baqara 2:125.

[4] Baqara 2:127.

5 Baqara 2:125.

6 Al Imran 3:97.

7 Tabari, l, 259; Ibn al-Athir, ibid. 1, 107.

8 *See* Ibn Kathir, *Tafsir*, 3,395.

9 *See* Tabari, 1, 261-262.

10 Ibn al-Athir ibid. l, 106-107.

11 Tabari 1, 276.

12 Ghazali, Ihya (translated by Serdaroglu), l, 765-766.

13 Bukhari, *Anbiya*, 9, (4,174); Tabari 1, 251-252; *See* Ibn Hajar, *Fath al-Bari*, 7, 209.

14 Saffat 37:100

15 Prophet Abraham was unsure of the first two dreams, not knowing whether they were from Satan or not. The third time he was convinced that the dream came from God Almighty (Baydawi, ibid. 2,158).

16 A peripheral story: It seems the horns of the ram that was sacrificed in place of Ishmael were preserved through the centuries as a relic inside the Ka'ba. According to Abu Dawud, Prophet Muhammad ordered that the horns be covered with a piece of cloth during prayer times to prevent them from distracting people (Abu Dawud, Manasik, 95).

17 Baydawi, 2, 159.

18 Ajluni, *Kashf al-Khafa*, 1,199-200. According to Hakim and Dhahabi, this *hadith* is judged as authentic because it is related by so many sources. Of the "two sacrifices," the first was that of his ancestor Ishmael, the son of Abraham and the other was that of his father Abdullah. Abdulmuttalib, the Prophet's grandfather, made a vow to sacrifice one of his sons if God gave him ten sons. When he was granted his wish, his sons drew lots and Abdullah was the one chosen randomly to be sacrificed. But the leaders of the Quraysh, fearing this would become a tradition, decided he should sacrifice camels instead. This is why Prophet Muhammad was proud to say "I am the son of two Sacrifices."

19 *See* Zukhruf 43:22-23, Baqara 2:170, Maidah 5:104.

20 There are several other verses of the Qur'an that refer to the imitation of ancestors as an excuse for paganism.

21 *Ijtihad* means, after acquiring the required knowledge and competence, deducing rules of law through juristic reasoning from original sources—the Qur'an and Sunna—if they present no decisive ruling on a particular matter. (Tr.)

22 Razi, *Tafsir* 25, 56.

23 Baqara 2:286.

24 Baqara 2:249.

25 Tabari, *History* 1, 234.

26 Suyuti, *al-Jami al-Saghir*, 3,71.

27   Razi, *Tafsir*, 21, 227.

28   As I mentioned earlier, Prophet Abraham was 37 years old when he emigrated. Since he emigrated immediately after his people tried to burn him in the fire, it is clear he had had no success up to this point.

29   Nursi, S., *The Words*, "The Twentieth Word," The Light, Inc., New Jersey: 2005, p. 273.

30   Nursi, S., *The Letters*, "The Twenty-Fourth Letter," Truestar, London: 1995.

31   Ibid.

32   Muslim, *Salat*, 226; Nasai, *Tatbik*, 79.

PART FOUR
THE CONTENTS OF THE PROPHET
ABRAHAM'S TEACHINGS

1   *See* Najm 53:36-37.

2   *... human has only that for which he labors.* (Najm 53:39)

3   Najm 53: 36-54

4   Ala 87:14-19

5   *See* Suyuti, *Durr al-Mansur*, 6, 341; Haqim, *Mustadraq*, 2, 425.

6   Tabari, *History* 1, 313.

7   Ibid.

8   Suyuti, *Durr al-Mansur*, 6, 341; Shahristani, *al-Milal*, 2, 47.

9   The fact that Prophet Abraham obeyed a divine command to come to Mecca does not contradict this statement, as it cannot be said that God did not have a purpose in giving this ethical guidance.

10   Muhammad ibn Muhammad, *Jam al-Fawaid*, Medina, 1961, 1, 1781 (h 1241).

11   Ibn Kathir, Tafsir, 2, 543.

12   Ibn Manzur, 10, 394.

13   Malek Bennabi, *Perspectives Algeriennes*, Algeria, 1964, p. 41, 43.

14   Abu Dawud, *Jihad*, 104; Nasai, *Qasama*, 25, (8, 36).

15   Dhariyat 51:56-57.

16   Bediüzzaman says that this verse *"teaches that one must not neglect worship under the pretext of breadwinning"* (The Rays Collection, 28th Ray, Sozler Publishing, Istanbul: 2000).

17   Al Imran 3:191.

18   Suyuti, *al-Jami al-Saghir*, 4, 248.

19   Bukhari, *Anbiya*, 8.

20   Ibrahim 14:40.

21   Saffat 37:100.

22   Ustrusani, *Ahkam al-Sigar*, 1, 215-216.

23 Ibn Hajar, *Fath al-Bari*, 6, 212.
24 *See* Tahrim 66:6; Shura 42:45; Zumar 39:15.
25 Saffat 37:106.
26 Zumar 39:15; Hajj 22:11.
27 Najm 53:37.
28 Tabari, 1,253-254.
29 Al-Kamil, 1,104.
30 Tabari, 1, 256.
31 Al-Kamil, 1, 104.
32 *See* Bukhari, Anbiya, 9; Tabari, 1, 256-257; al-Kamil, 1, 104-105.
33 Mumtahana 60:4.
34 Shuara 26:86.
35 Tawba 9:84.
36 *See* Tabari, ibid, 1, 255; Ibn al-Athir, *al-Kamil*, 1, 103.
37 Tabari, ibid, 1, 288; *al-Kamil*, 1,112.
38 Tabari, 1, 275.
39 Hud 11:13.
40 Tabari, ibid, 1, 274.
41 Ibn Athir, ibid, 1, 111-112.

PART FIVE
THE PROPHET ABRAHAM'S EXEMPLARY STRUGGLE

1   Anbiya 21:69; Saffat 37:88-113
2   Ankabut 29:26.
3   Razi, *Tafsir*, 20,135.
4   Shuara 26:214.
5   Luqman 31:13-19.
6   Hud 11:45.
7   Muslim, *Qadar*, 1.
8   Razi, *Tafsir*, 13, 48.
9   As Prophet Noah was boarding the ark and urging the believers to embark, he also cried out to one of his sons, "O my dear son! Embark with us, and remain not with those who deny the truth!" But the son answered, "I shall betake myself to a mountain that will protect me from the waters," and rejected his father's plea, preferring to resist with the unbelievers, and thus was among those who drowned. (Hud 11:42-43)
10 Tahrim 66:10. The same verse likens Prophet Lot's wife to Prophet Noah's wife.
11 Razi, ibid. 13, 49.
12 Razi, ibid. 13,48.

13 Razi, ibid. 13, 57.
14 Maryam 19:42-47.
15 *See* Ankabut 29:25, 61-63; Zumar 39:38; Zukhruf 43:9; 87; Ibrahim 14:9-10.
16 *See* Ibn abi Shayba 1,348; Abdurrazzaq, 4,334.
17 Saffat 37:88-90.
18 Ankabut 29:26.
19 Tabari, ibid. 1, 239.
20 Musnad 2, 406, 437, 482-83.
21 Ibn Maja, *Fitan*, 33, 4077.

BIBLIOGRAPHY

Abdul Razzaq al-San'ani, *Musannaf*, Beirut, 1970.

Al-Ajluni, *Kashf al-Khafa*.

Ahmad ibn Hanbal, al-*Musnad*.

Rogers Bastide, *Eléments de sociologie religieuse*, Armand Colin, Paris: 1947.

Said Nursi, *Hutba al-Shamiya* (The Damascus Sermon), Envar Neşriyat, Istanbul: 1990.

- *Isharat al-Ijaz* (The Signs of Miraculousness), Ankara, 1979.
- *The Flashes Collection*, Sozler Publications, Istanbul: 2000.
- *The Letters*, Kaynak, Izmir: 1998.
- *Munazarat* (Discussions), Istanbul: 1991.
- *Risale-i Nur Kulliyati* (Risale-i Nur Collection), Nesil Yayinlari, Istanbul: 1994.
- *The Words*, The Light, Inc., New Jersey: 2005.
- *Sualar* (The Rays), Sozler Publications, Istanbul: 1992.

Baydawi, *Tafsir*, vol. II, Egypt, 1955.

Sahih al-Bukhari, Cairo, 1958.

Ibrahim Canan, *Hangi Medeniyet, Hangi Kültür*, Yeni Asya, Istanbul: 1996.

- *Peygamberimizin Teblig Metotlari* (The Prophet's Methods of Communication)- 1 - 2, Nesil, Istanbul: 1998.
- *Islamda Cocuk Haklari* (Children's Rights in Islam), Yeni Asya, Istanbul, 1980.
- *Islam Aleminin Ana Meselelerine Bediuzzaman'dan Cozumler* (Solutions from Bediuzzaman for the Main Problems of Muslims), Yeni Asya, 1993.
- *Islamda Temel Egitim Esaslari* (Basics of Education in Islam), Yeni Asya, Istanbul: 1980.
- *Kur'an'da Cocuk Egitimi* (Children's Education in the Qur'an), Nesil, Istanbul: 1996.

- *Kutub-i Sitte Muhtasari Tercume ve Serhi* (The Translation and Explanation of The Six Books of Hadith), Akçag, Ankara: 1993.
- *Teblig Terbiye ve Siyasi Taktik Acilarindan Hicret* (The Emigration with respect to Communicating the Message, Education, and Political Strategy), Yeni Asya y. Ist. 1981.

Diyanet Vakfi Islam Ansiklopedisi (Encyclopedia of Islam), Turkish Presidency of Religious Affairs, Istanbul.

Abu Dawud, *Sunan* (with annotations from Hattabi),Homs: 1969.

Mircea Eliade, *Traité d'histoire des religions*, PAOT, Paris: 1970.

Hamdi Yazir of Elmali, *Tafsir*, 2nd ed., Istanbul: 1960.

L'Encyclopédie de l'Islâm, lst ed.

Imam Ghazali, *Ihya Ulum al-Din*, trans. Ahmet Serdaroglu, Istanbul: 1975.

Al-Hakim, *al-Mustadrak*.

Ali Ibn Burhaneddin Halabi, *Sirat al-Halebiyya*, Beirut.

Muhammad Hamidullah, *Islam Peygamberi* (The Prophet of Islam), Istanbul: 1990.

Nureddin Haythami, *Majma al-Zawaid*, Beirut: 1967.

Abdullah ibn Ebi Jamra, *Bahjat al-Nufus*, 2nd ed., Beirut, 1972.

Izzeddin ibn al-Athir, *al-Kamil fi't-Tarikh*, Beirut: 1965.

Majdeddin ibn al-Athir, *Al-Nihayafi Garib al-Hadith wa'l-Asar*, Cairo: 1963.

Izzeddin Ibn al-Athir, *Usd al-Ghaba*, Cairo:1970.

Ibn Hajar, *Fath al-Bari*, Egypt, 1952.

- *Al-Matalib al-Aliya*, Quwait, 1973.

Ibn Hazm al-Zahiri, *al-Fasl fi'l-Milal wa'n-Nihal*, 2nd ed., Beirut: 1975.

Ibn Kathir, *an-Nihayafi'l-Fitan wa'l-Malahim*, Cairo:1969.

- *Tafsir*, Beirut: 1966.

Ibn Maja, *Sunan*,Tahqiq: M. F. Abdul Baqi, Cairo: l952.

Ibn Sa'd, *Tabaqat al-Kubra*, Beirut: 1960.

Islam Ansiklopedisi, Turkish Ministry of Education: Istanbul.

Kitab-i Mukaddes (The Bible), Eski ve Yeni Ahid (The Old and New Testaments), Istanbul:1958.

Razi ibn Umar, *Tafsir al-Kabir*, Cairo.

Malik ibn Anas, *Muwatta*, Tahqiq, M.F. Abdul Baqi, Cairo:1951.

Malek Bennabi, *Perspectives Algeriennes, Algeria*, 1964.

Mu'jam al-Buldan, see Ya'qub al-Hamawi.

Muhammad ibn Muhammad, *Jam al-Fawaid*, Medina: 1961.

Abdul Rauf Al-Munawi, *Fayz al-Qadr*, Sharh al-Jami al-Saghir, Beirut: 1972.

Sahih al-Muslim, Tahqiq, M. F. Abdulbaqi, Cairo:1955.

Nasai, Ahmad ibn Ali, *Sunan*, Cairo: 1930.

Maxime Rodinson, *Mahomet*, Seuil, Paris: 1961.

Muhammad Ali Al-Sabuni, *Saffat al-Tafasir*, vol. 4, Beirut, 1981.

Sarahsi, Muhammad ibn Ahmad, *Usul al-Sarahsi*, Beirut:1973.

Sayyid Qutb, *Fi Zilal al-Qur'an*, Istanbul: 1979.

Suyuti, Jalaleddin, *al-Jami al-Saghir*, Beirut:1972.

      – *Tafsir al-Jalalayn*, Damascus, 1378.

      – *Durr al-Mansur*, Beirut.

      – *Ziyada al-Jami al-Saghir*, Beirut.

Shahristani, Muhammad ibn Abdul Karim, *al-Milal wa'n-Nihal*, Beirut:1975.

Tabari, *Tarih al-Tabari*, Tahqiq: Muhammad Abu'l-Fadl, Lebanon.

Tirmidhi, *Sunan al-Tirmidhi*, Ta'liq: Aziz Ubayd, Homs, 1966.

Toynbee, *L'Histoire*, trans. Elisabeth Julia, Gallimard, Paris: 1961.

Osman Turan, *Turk Cihan Hakimiyeti Mefkuresi Tarihi*, Istanbul: 1969.

Muhammad Usrushani, Ahkam al-Sighar, Egypt.

Yaqub al-Hamawi, Mu'jam al-Buldan, Beirut, 1957.

Muhammad ibn Abdul Baqi Zurqani, *Sharh al-Mawaqib al-Ladunniya*, Beirut: 1973.

INDEX